THE McCANN YEARS

THE McCANN YEARS
The Inside Story of Celtic's Revolution

Allan Caldwell

MAINSTREAM
PUBLISHING
EDINBURGH AND LONDON

First published in Great Britain in 1999 by
MAINSTREAM PUBLISHING COMPANY (EDINBURGH) LTD
7 Albany Street
Edinburgh EH1 3UG

ISBN 1 84018 115 X

A catalogue record for this book is available from the British Library

Typeset in Berkeley Book
Printed and bound in Great Britain by Creative Print and Design Wales

CONTENTS

ACKNOWLEDGEMENTS

Thanks to the following for their valuable assistance:

The *Evening Times* (Scottish Media Group) and *The Sun*.
Brian Dempsey, Willie Haughey, Dominic Keane and
David Murray; Eddie Keane and 'The Bhoys from
Bermuda'. Thanks also to Jim Farry and Frank Cairney.
   A special thanks to Lorraine for her support and patience.
Likewise to my daughters Sharon and Sarah Jane.

As he left Celtic Park, Dempsey turned and looked back at the stadium point. A new era was indeed dawning, he thought. But what will it bring? What would people expect? Expect? He laughed to himself. Never expect anything, particularly if it has anything to do with Celtic Football Club.

Taken from the final page of Allan Caldwell's
Sack the Board, 1994

ONE

The Deal

IT had been a long, exhausting day. It was now becoming an even longer one. The rebels had already secured victory and only one man – one of the defiant Old Guard – remained, awaiting his pieces of silver.

Celtic director Michael Kelly hadn't only sold out the others, he'd sold out himself. Or, at least, he was in the process of doing so. So many years of the Kelly dynasty were resting now on the shoulders of one person, and it was all down to money.

Fergus John McCann, 53, the least likely of the Celtic saviours – his small, thin, bespectacled appearance belying the aggressive, arrogant character living within – was seething. He didn't want to pay 'one single dime' to the last remaining director to hold out on his shareholding. The fact that Michael Kelly, the former Lord Provost of Glasgow, personally held very few shares did not cut any ice with McCann.

Bonnet-wearing McCann – son of a headmaster from the former mining village of Croy in Central Scotland – had been absent from the country of his birth for around thirty years. But, as he concentrated on making his millions in Canada, America and Bermuda, he had built up a reputation as a shrewd – if rather secretive – individual. Now he was back. Swept into a position of power with the help of the rebel forces back home led by former Celtic director and Glasgow-based businessman Brian Dempsey.

McCann, or the old Bhoy from Croy as he was to become known, was in no mood to compromise – a trait later to lead to bitter clashes within the club and much, much further afield.

The growing crowd of supporters outside Celtic Park was becoming increasingly impatient despite having sensed that the rebels were already in control.

Inside the bright corridors of Celtic power, that sense of the long-awaited control was also evident. But, rather than Michael Kelly being the stumbling block, it was now Fergus McCann.

Glasgow accountant, Dominic Keane, was the rebel who had been chosen to thrash out the deal with Michael Kelly. Brian Dempsey could not negotiate it as he and Kelly had no time for each other; Kelly had been instrumental in having Dempsey axed from the Celtic board shortly after the two had been appointed four years earlier. Keane had been locked in a side-room at Celtic Park with the last remaining director of the former board yet to agree terms for the sale of his and his family's shares.

Keane had been enlisted by the rebels early in the fight and he also represented his brother – former Glasgow carpet king, Eddie, who was now a tax exile living in Bermuda.

Eddie was one of the Scottish investors who formed the consortium with Dempsey, his business partner John Keane (no relation to Eddie or Dominic), McCann and publican Jack Flannigan.

Michael Kelly's resolve not to sell out had been broken weeks earlier when a second consortium, backed by former Glasgow stores magnate Gerald Weisfeld and led by his stepson Michael McDonald and city businessman

Willie Haughey, had the old board split over their substantial cash offer for their shares.

Their bid had failed due to the infamous 'pact of five' which had bound the top five Celtic directors to an agreement that they must first offer shares to each other before a third party could buy them.

Dempsey supporters, Kevin Kelly and Tom Grant, had invoked that pact to stop the others selling out to Weisfeld. But it had the desired effect of breaking Michael Kelly, and now it was all down to how much he could get.

Dominic Keane finally emerged from the room looking jubilant. He had managed to broker a deal with Michael Kelly. The day was now surely won. Not for one moment did he expect the reaction he got from McCann. The little Scots–Canadian blew a fuse. Under no circumstances did he want Kelly cashing in at his expense. In McCann's eyes Kelly was beaten and had no way out. But in Dempsey's eyes, McCann was blind.

Dempsey hauled McCann into the boot-room. They emerged a short time later. The deal *was* done and Keane was told to go back into the room where Kelly was and tie it up.

The events of that day, Friday, 4 March, were not for the faint-hearted. As Dominic Keane recalled: 'Fergus was still in Canada at this time and had only publicly come into our group in the latter six or nine months. Previously, all the hard work in getting the shares together and pooling all the resources was done by Brian Dempsey. It was his vision to bring other key members into the consortium at the appropriate time.

'When we reached the last couple of days, there were many phone calls between Glasgow and the Caribbean, where Brian was on a working holiday in Grand Cayman. Instructions were being taken as to what we should do next. It was agreed that because we were getting to the final points where there was no way forward for the old board,

I should phone McCann and tell him that we thought it would be all over soon and that the club would be in our control by Friday.

'So, on that basis, McCann booked his ticket and flew over. On the day of the takeover there was a great furore outside the park when McCann appeared. There were hundreds, probably even thousands outside, and negotiations were still going on inside. We wanted to get this thing over, and the only way was to broker a deal with the remaining directors, of which Michael Kelly was the last to hold out. Although we didn't want to pay money for their shares, it was clear in the real world deals had to be done whether we liked them or not.

'So, when McCann arrived that morning, I was in with Michael Kelly trying to finalise a deal with his shares and those of his family group. I remember coming out and feeling quite good. It had been tough but having secured a very favourable price, I felt we had reached a conclusion and the final piece in the jigsaw which gave us way over the 50 per cent we needed.

'I think Smith was there as well. Michael Kelly was extremely awkward but we explained to him that we already had directors Tom Grant and Jack McGinn with us, along with Jimmy Farrell, and there was no way he could hold us back.

'But he was holding out for a reasonable price for the shares. That's all that mattered at that point, just how much he was getting. The Celtic issues were all resolved. Celtic, in my view, was the furthest thing from his mind. If you wanted control of this club then there was a price to pay; we had to negotiate a price which we could live with and Kelly thought was fair as well.

'I remember coming out of that meeting in the boardroom – just outside where the players' room is – and Brian appeared and asked how things were going. I said: "I think we've got a deal, though it's a bit more than we would have expected. But, at the end of the day, we can go outside and tell the people it's all over." Brian seemed pretty happy with that.

'At that point, McCann appeared and asked what was going on. We told him we'd just made a deal on the Michael Kelly shares. Amazingly McCann wanted to call it off there and then.

'He said: "These guys are not getting a penny." He had only just appeared and within minutes an argument was blazing between myself, Brian and Fergus about whether shares owned by the existing board should be purchased or not.

'I put it down to him maybe being tired as he'd flown through the night after a long trip. The reality was that they had to sell, and we wanted to buy as many of these shares as possible to get control. Brian Dempsey was probably the best one to negotiate with Michael Kelly, but he couldn't – there was too much bad feeling between them. Brian thought it was better for another member of the consortium to go in and negotiate. That job fell to me. I felt at that time, bearing in mind that we had to move quickly, that it was all very well saying that the club would have gone down, the shares would have been worth nothing and we could have waited, but this thing could have been prolonged. It was not the sort of situation you could take the risk with. It was a game of poker and, at the end of the day, I think there were really no other options.

'Anyway, Brian took Fergus aside and had a private word with him – I don't know what he said although I've got a good idea – and within minutes Brian came back and said: "Well done, Dominic. That's a good deal you've done and that's the final piece in the jigsaw." Within half an hour we were on the front steps of Celtic Park after agreeing a statement from all the old board and the new regime.

'But I'll never forget how close it came after the reaction from Fergus. At one point it could all have been off with him saying we are not going to pay this, we are not going to pay that. He almost jeopardised the deal as soon as he walked through the door.'

Dempsey couldn't quite remember exactly what words were exchanged between himself and McCann, but he's in no doubt they were heated.

With so much at stake, reasoning with someone like McCann required skill, authority and aggression.

Dempsey recalled: 'Fergus didn't want to give them a dime, as he put it; he thought we could get away without paying anything. The discussions had taken place already. Dominic went in and spoke to David Smith and Michael Kelly and I took Fergus and went into the boot-room at Celtic Park and convinced him and Charles Barnett [from Fergus's financial advisers Panell Kerr], that it was the right thing to do as it secured the club.

'Up to that point, you put money in with no guarantee that they could have locked the Emergency General Meeting; they could have done anything. But a deal allowed us to go through the EGM in control of the club. Fergus did not want to part with any money. I am not saying it was right or wrong, but our way was the safer way, the more expensive way, but the safer way, and it was money that won the day.

'McCann wasn't happy, but David Smith was the man who convinced the others to take the money and go. He was the man who convinced them they were beaten – they were finished and they couldn't recover from this. Outside, the fans were stunned and the old board could not face them. The ousted directors had to be taken out by the back door and well away from the stadium as there were hundreds and hundreds of fans at the front door. It was approaching midnight and the crowd was growing bigger by the hour. Michael Kelly was the last one to go. To his credit he came round to every one of us and shook hands and said congratulations. Fergus said to him words to the effect that he should have gone a long time ago.'

The war had been won and, like any type of human conflict, it had taken its toll. Leaders had emerged and so too had the inner characters of the players involved.

Fergus McCann was not happy with the way they had achieved surrender. For him the war was over – but a new battle had already begun.

BRIAN DEMPSEY had never been close to Fergus McCann, despite what others thought during the build-up to the rebel take over. Most of their contact was by fax and telephone as McCann was thousands of miles away at his apartment in Montreal, his golfing breaks in Arizona or his second home in Bermuda.

Dempsey had travelled over to meet McCann a few times and McCann had come to Glasgow. Both claimed to have Celtic at heart, but that is where the similarities began and ended.

One of the few, private occasions they had was shortly before the take over when Dempsey invited McCann to his house for dinner.

The object of the dinner was more business than pleasure. Dempsey was teetotal and liked to stay focused on the matter in hand – even over a meal. McCann liked the odd drink and enjoyed a glass of wine. But it was difficult to keep McCann's attention when he was not the one doing the talking.

That night, Dempsey began to press a few points home regarding the plan of attack. He was astounded when McCann lay down on the carpet and began doing a series of stretching exercises.

Dempsey stared at him. He thought: 'What a really

eccentric way to behave in someone's home!' It wasn't as if they were the best of friends. The host looked down at his guest and asked: 'I assume our discussion is over?'

McCann replied: 'Yeah, I guess so. Time I went home.' It was McCann's first and last visit to the Dempsey household.

Now that control of Celtic Football Club was firmly in the hands of the new shareholders, Dempsey noticed the changes which had been developing in this eccentric little man were now fairly obvious for all to see. And he didn't like what he saw.

The two had fallen out on what should have been a glorious, victorious day in the history of Celtic. That fall-out was growing. The gulf between the two instigators in the battle for control was quickly becoming too wide to bridge.

McCann was the biggest investor with just over £7 million ready to be put into the club – with the other five investors ready to inject £1 million each – and that gave him the edge.

Something had to go. That something was Brian Dempsey. He chose to walk away rather than see the fruits of their labours disintegrate around them in a public battle, as that would do the club, the players and the faithful supporters no good.

After only a week the pair had been arguing on a daily basis. McCann then refused to be photographed beside Dempsey after a meeting inside Celtic Park.

A few days later Dempsey was outraged when he went into McCann's office at Celtic Park and found him surrounded by 'advisers', apparently making decisions regarding the club without discussing it with the rest of the investors. Dempsey had promised to invest £1 million – if the correct and agreed policies were to be implemented. McCann offered him a seat on the board, but the Glasgow businessman refused. He was still unsure about McCann and his promises. Dempsey headed abroad on business while McCann denied any rift between them. But the paperwork between the two and their lawyers told a different story.

The first broadside came from Dempsey in response to a letter from McCann on 10 March – only six days after the take over – offering Dempsey a seat on the board. The offer was conditional on Dempsey investing £1 million as he and the other Scottish investors had agreed. But it was the manner in which McCann offered him the directorship and the way he outlined how he saw Dempsey's role – mainly that of a figurehead for the media and the supporters – which infuriated him.

Dempsey replied immediately. The letter gave a quite uncanny view into the future.

He wrote: 'Your letter which you sent without discussion with your board in no way addresses the real problems and real issues facing Celtic Football Club.

'Firstly, the discussion with yourself, Dominic [Keane] and Raymond Blinn [an independent financial adviser] was distasteful in that Raymond Blinn has no locus whatsoever in this matter – a matter for Celtic directors and share-holders, notwithstanding supporters – and that discussion demonstrated to me fully that accountants, lawyers and the like are the type of people you wish around you.

'Sycophancy is not one of my strong points but I regret to say you depend on it.

'May I remind you that all these "advisers" were paid by a group and not by you alone, and they are responsible to that group and not to you alone.

'May I also remind you that you instructed an audit without the consent of this investor group, never mind the directors of Celtic Football Club, nor have you made any meaningful attempt to have any type of discussion with your comrades but only with your "advisers". I believe this has been wrong and will rebound on you.'

Dempsey then turned his attention to the matters relating to himself included in the letter.

He wrote: 'Let me say that the Celtic support has responded in a magnificent way over these last three and a half years – as have many others directly and indirectly involved in Celtic. The important issues within our football club now range over broader issues more fundamental to ensuring that what happened before will never happen again.

'This embraces many matters which the Celtic support has knowledge and understanding of and wishes to have knowledge and understanding of. Only then will they be prepared to purchase shares in their football club in the full knowledge that the people in charge are good Celtic people and the advice given comes from good Celtic people.

'That is not the case at this time. I warned you that one ego trip would not be replaced by another and that is the manner in which you have begun – and must be stopped.'

Dempsey went on to stress that his own contribution had been greater than McCann's in terms of 'time, energy, commitment and constancy'. He described references to him by McCann as 'insulting' and said the Scottish investors' group would have to meet and ask questions.

Those questions included whether the group was still prepared to invest, if it was happy with the 'management-style manner' in which McCann appeared to want to run the club, and if the Weisfeld consortium should be asked in to enlarge the capital base and, more importantly, introduce more 'Celtic people' rather than advisers.

Dempsey added: 'I note how and when you see my "increasing involvement", which I presume means – in my style of English – that I keep the media and the fans sweet – running on the back of my credibility – while you and your "advisers" decide exactly what, how, where and when all the issues confronting Celtic are decided. Not on your life! The Celtic support and the media deserve the truth and I intend to ensure that always is the case.

'I do not believe these overall decisions should be made by you alone, and I most certainly do not approve that they are made by your "advisers" who have no experience of the traditions that are Celtic.'

In relation to the offer of a directorship on that basis, Dempsey concluded: 'My answer to you is a firm no.'

It was a further month before the two started talking again, but only in relation to the investors' group.

Dempsey's next move was through his lawyer. He wrote to McCann proposing to commit his initial £1 million investment in shares, but on the basis that McCann and Dempsey could agree a satisfactory deal over Dempsey's involvement.

The lawyer wrote: 'I have had a number of discussions with Brian regarding his interest in the club and his possible investment therein and his relationship with yourself and others at Celtic Park.

'Without going into the latter in detail, it is clear that there have been major difficulties between the two of you since the takeover.

'If you feel there is no future for Brian either as an investor or a director then I think this should be made clear now to avoid any further time-wasting.'

McCann responded a few days later on 24 May claiming Dempsey had reneged on his original investment deal and had already turned down a directorship. He said he was willing to sell him some of his own shares – but only if Dempsey acknowledged McCann's leadership abilities.

McCann wrote: 'Not only has the investor group been represented by a director [John Keane] prior to them providing any funding or even a loan portion, this appointment was at the request of Brian Dempsey.

'Since that time, an additional board appointment was offered to him which he declined. When the [rights] offer closed and the music stopped at 12 noon last Friday a total of £12.4 million of underwriting was produced and accepted by the Celtic board. I was disappointed to see that no funds were in place from Mr Dempsey – or any signed underwriting letter.

'So, quite naturally, I am curious to see in your letter the new conditions and a reversal of the concept of a lead investor. It suggests that most of the commitment to invest follows public subscription instead of leading it . . .

'As things presently stand, if Brian wishes to purchase shares from me I will be agreeable to sell them to him at the current price of £60 a share.

'This could only be treated as an investment decision on its own merits, i.e. confidence in the club's present and future prospects, my own abilities and commitments and comfort with the overall plans to be implemented.'

McCann said he welcomed Dempsey 'as a major public and private supporter' but ruled out a directorship, concluding: 'I will sell shares to any suitable buyer but not in the contractual way you outline; investing and management, although related, are distinctly different.'

Dempsey admitted defeat. He realised he had missed the boat. The reply from Dempsey's lawyer was conciliatory.

Dempsey accepted the question of investment and management should be kept separate and said he was still prepared to invest £1 million by taking up unallocated shares or by taking up McCann's offer to sell him some of his own.

The question of a directorship – and the remit of it – being up to current directors and shareholders 'if there is a vacancy'.

McCann, realising he was winning this skirmish, again adopted a dismissive tone.

He wrote back saying all the relevant shares were taken up and effectively withdrew his offer to sell some of his own shares saying: 'To sell £1 million of shares to Brian now would help me financially but would dilute my controlling interest in the club.

'I am reluctant to do this and all the other major investors prefer that I maintain a controlling position which provides stability to the club at this important time.'

He suggested Dempsey could invest his £1 million when the public share offer came out, 'assuming it was not oversubscribed'.

McCann also added a 'P.S.' accusing Dempsey of stirring the issue in the press and creating a 'negative distraction' from the task of rebuilding the club.

But before that letter reached its destination, Dempsey had already had second thoughts.

McCann had been guilty of airing matters through the media and, on the same day (13 June) that McCann's letter was posted, it crossed with another from Dempsey's lawyer.

Dempsey's brief wrote: 'My instructions have been overtaken by events in the press.' It referred to a story in the *Evening Times* in which McCann had taken a public swipe at Dempsey's 'non-investment' in the club.

A story also appeared in *The Sun* – from Celtic sources – linking Dempsey with the chairmanship of the club.

The letter from Dempsey's lawyer continued: 'Both Brian and I are in no doubt that these stories are being raised to cause an unbreachable rift between you and Brian and to preclude him from any meaningful part in the future of Celtic.

'It is clear to Brian and to his advisers that he should not go where he is not wanted. You will appreciate that having gone through a traumatic three years he has not taken this decision lightly.'

Dempsey withdrew his offer of £1 million investment. His association with the club would continue through sponsorship and hospitality and he would continue to be a thorn in McCann's flesh.

But McCann had shown from day one the ruthless and dictatorial streak which was to become his feared trademark and, more often, the one which was also to become his own worst enemy.

TWO

The Man McCann

THE first few days at Celtic Park were strange, new and, at times, more than a little scary for Fergus McCann. There was intense media interest in him and all that was happening at Celtic. McCann had said from day one that the club would be 'more open' and that he would not hide away from journalists and their questions. But already he was beginning to regret his pledge. The cramming of reporters and photographers along with radio microphones and television cameras into his new office at Celtic Park was becoming a bit of a burden. How many times could he be asked to read out goodwill cards from supporters and pose with a big, cheesy grin? Particularly when he seldom had cause or the inclination to attempt a big, cheesy grin.

His small frame, unfortunate squint and the bunnet which rarely left his balding head, didn't give him with the best photographic attributes.

It became apparent then that McCann had maybe bitten off a little more than he could chew. He certainly hadn't anticipated the media circus which surrounded and hounded him.

Just before Brian Dempsey's short spell at the club with the new owner reached an end, the two men had dealt with one of the first real media problems to strike.

Dempsey had heard from press contacts that a Sunday tabloid newspaper had dispatched an investigative team to Canada to look into the relatively unknown background of Fergus John McCann. Rather than shrug it off or simply call the newspaper and answer any questions, McCann appeared to panic. It made Dempsey wonder if there was a skeleton in the cupboard that the little Scots–Canadian wanted to keep hidden.

Dempsey called in a sports news reporter he knew and asked if he could offer any advice to McCann.

The journalist asked McCann if he had anything to hide. The reaction was again surprising.

McCann said: 'I don't want anyone looking into my personal life. Why would they want to do that? What are they trying to find?' He refused to answer the initial question.

The journalist suggested McCann should wait and see if anything emerged from the investigation but advised him to contact people back in his adopted home to advise them of the situation.

After a few months nothing did appear in the press. That's when the journalist decided to investigate McCann's background for himself.

His first reference point was a CV which McCann himself had written and presented to the old Celtic board some years previously when he first made an approach to the club offering to invest.

The typewritten, single sheet of paper was compiled by McCann while he sat in his rented apartment in Scottsdale, Arizona, during the spring of 1990. It was the place McCann liked to go to escape the harsh winters of Canada and enjoy some golf.

The CV read:

Scottsdale, 6 April 1990. Re: Fergus McCann. Some brief information about myself which may be helpful. Personal details at 31 March 1990.

Age 48. Single. Born Scotland. Canadian citizen. Reside Bermuda. [It then gave his addresses in Montreal (summer) and Bermuda.]

Background: Educated in Stirling and Glasgow. St Modans HS, St Aloysius Coll, Glasgow and Strathclyde Universities, Inst of CAs (chartered accountants). CA 1963. MBA 1968.

Career in Montreal 1963–82: Accounting and financial and management positions. Touche Ross, Cott Beverages, Seagram, Marconi. Lectured in management at McGill Univ 1969–74. Promoted Celtic v Inter Milan telecast Toronto, 1972.

The reference to the telecast match made no mention of the fact that it almost ruined McCann financially. The match was the European Cup semi-final. It had gone into extra time which McCann hadn't budgeted for when costing the satellite broadcast for a Celtic audience on screens at the Maple Leaf Gardens in Toronto. The match lasted 122 minutes – at a cost of 10,000 Canadian dollars per hour plus overheads.

The CV continued:

Started International Golf Inc 1973. World Golf Management, Bermuda 1982. Sold these companies to ADT in 1986.

Presently: Operates the Firstgreen Foundation (charitable) in Canada, some golf travel consulting and personal investment company (Bermuda).

Held various meetings with Celtic officials over last two years regarding investment/marketing/management proposals.

Personal investment company: Firstgreen Ltd. Diversified portfolio – no debt. Home in Bermuda.

> Objective: Long-term investment, management and marketing role in the development of Celtic Football Club's business and park.

He omitted to mention that he was brought up in Kilsyth and that his father, Allen, was headmaster of the local school; that he had three sisters and was a former treasurer of the Croy Celtic Supporters' Club.

Brief details for a man who packed his bags and left Croy for Canada after – according to Dempsey – having informed his parents only the night before he left.

But it was enough for the journalist to pick up the McCann trail. First stop: Canada.

MONTREAL is the second-biggest French-speaking city in the world and is home to a large Catholic community. It is regarded as the greatest inland port on earth and sits beside the St Lawrence River. It is also a very cosmopolitan city with the *joie de vivre* of the French Quarter contrasting with the American get-up-and-go.

The old and the new sit together with the crest of Gothic buildings and stately residences reflected in the glass of the tall, modern office blocks, and with more street cafés and bars than almost any other North American city.

It may not boast a top 'soccer' team, but it does have one of the best stadiums. The Skydome is even bigger and better than Celtic Park.

French–Canadian Jean Cyr is a concierge at the sprawling apartment block in Montreal's east end where McCann lived. His opinion and stories about the Bhoy from Croy offer a unique insight into the man who took over one of Britain's biggest clubs.

McCann worked as an accountant with several firms in Canada before setting up a business operating golf tours around Scotland. After a few years, his business was booming with rich Canadians and Americans paying top prices for the specialised tours.

Often he would come over with them and play some golf himself. Other times local people would act as 'tour guides'.

He then sold the business for a sum believed to be around £5 million and then began investing in various fields operating from his plush appartment in Montreal.

Jean Cyr, the tall, poker-faced doorman, revealed another side to McCann: the fits of pique McCann had and the shouting matches with staff at the apartments. The bright flats at 4300 Maisonneuve are built along a tree-lined avenue in the Westmont.

McCann lived in the city for several years and rented suite 430 at Maisonneuve for two years until he gave up his lease shortly after the Celtic take over. He was described as being very much a loner with visitors seemingly restricted to a male friend, a succession of middle-aged women, believed to be agency secretaries, and occasional visits from his elderly mother who had moved out to Canada after the death of her husband.

Of the female visitors, Jean said: 'They were regular-looking women, medium. Not models or anything and not the women-of-the night type, either. All were middle-aged. I do not know why they were here, but I never saw them staying the night. I start at 7 a.m. and they were never here then.'

As well as the female visitors, McCann's mystery male friend was about the only other regular visitor. Jean described the friend as 'around the same age as McCann, tall with fair hair, who lives near the apartment block'.

He was a freqent visitor and collected mail for McCann when he was away on his travels. Jean continued 'He was a very good friend. He had the key to go into the house, water the plants and everything. He lives around here, but I don't know where. When McCann was away this man would be here every week to pick up the mail and any parcels.

'When McCann was here, this man used to come a few times, but McCann was gone a lot of the time. There were only a few other visitors and we had to call him to let him know who they were before they were allowed to go upstairs.'

Several Brits live in the block. Most are friendly and chat with staff, but not McCann. Jean remembered vividly the rumpus McCann caused shortly after his arrival. He said: 'McCann drove, a red BMW I think. I remember he drove to the front door and stopped. This is where the taxis stop and deliveries are made. We have a garage for the residents which is closed late at night, after that they leave their cars and the guy in the garage parks them.

But McCann parked his car right at the front and locked the door. The gateman told him not to leave it there, but McCann said: "I live here, I'll put it where I want." Then he went upstairs. He caused a problem and the doorman was in trouble because this is the driveway for the local taxis.

'He went to McCann's door and knocked but McCann wouldn't answer. The next morning the superintendent went upstairs to tell him to put his car in the garage. McCann banged the door in the superintendent's face and then eventually came downstairs yelling. He's a very strange man.

'But if somebody is not very nice to me it does not matter, I treat them all the same. I think he realised this when his mother came here for two weeks' vacation. I was helping her into the car as she had a lot of trouble walking. I think he started to think about what he was doing to us, the way he treated us.

'But he was all for himself. He didn't talk to us. He had money, his own business, but he did not want anyone to know about it. He was a lonely man.'

According to Jean, McCann seldom spoke to neighbours in the apartments and had few friends. He is also unknown in prominent financial circles in Montreal, and even the local media knew nothing of him. It was only when calls started to come in from the media in Scotland that the *Montreal Gazette* became aware of Fergus McCann. They ran one story under the headline: MONTREALER EYES GLASGOW CELTIC: 'ECCENTRIC' MILLIONAIRE WANTS TO BUY FAMOUS CLUB. The story, in the sports section, was quickly forgotten.

McCann's ventures at night were equally quiet and almost unnoticed. He sometimes used a local taxi company to take him about a mile and a half into the city to the trendy restaurant area around Rue Sherbrooke. One taxi driver who picked McCann up several times remembers dropping him off at the same spot – an upmarket restaurant on Sherbrooke at its junction with Peel. Close by is the sleazy side of Montreal – the strip joints, gay bars and sex shops. It's an area full of prostitutes, pimps and drug dealers. A neon village catering for all tastes, and a world apart from the top restaurants on Sherbrooke, which effectively marks the boundary line between good taste and bad.

By day, McCann, when not involved in business or trips abroad, spent his time on the golf course. He joined a golf course across the St Lawrence River to the south of Montreal, which was built on an Indian reservation. McCann was listed as a non-resident member in the 1994 Kanawaki Golf Club members' book. His office telephone number was given as the one in Montreal, while his home number was not in Glasgow, despite having moved back, but was for his apartment in Bermuda which he had rented out. The mystery surrounding McCann was no clearer at his golf club. General manager of the club, Welshman and former footballer, Tim Rees, was just as shocked as others when he learned of McCann's interest in

Celtic. He said: 'I know nothing about him. He's just a member here. I know he loves golf and that's about it. He travels a lot. He never talked about Celtic. When the members read about it in the paper they cut it out and put it on the noticeboard.

'I mentioned Celtic to him after that but he didn't say much. I understood what an enormous undertaking it was, but I don't think many local people understood what buying Celtic meant. But they were shocked about the amount of money being talked about. I think people thought he had been successful, but I didn't know if anyone thought he was a millionaire.

'I really don't know if he had any friends here. He wasn't here a great deal. He's a quiet man, unless he believes strongly in something. That's about all I know.' The only other thing Tim Rees now knows is that Fergus McCann is the only member to have attended the club's 75th anniversary dinner who did not appear in the photographs.

Three massive red volumes containing every face that came along – except McCann's. Tim added: 'That's strange. I gave instructions that everyone was to be photographed when they arrived but for some reason he is not among any of the pictures in the albums, yet I know he was here.'

CURIOUS was a word now firmly associated with McCann and his background. Toronto, the financial capital of eastern Canada, created even more curiosity.

McCann spent time, a lot of it, on business in Toronto – a city regarded as safe and clean, dwarfed under futuristic tower blocks, resting on an underworld city of shopping malls.

It seems that McCann, and, indeed, now Celtic, had a North American connection that few in the club were aware of. The man in question is a French Jew, brought up in Uruguay, now living in Canada and heavily involved in financial circles in Toronto. He is one of Celtic's biggest single investors. He is also an acquaintance of Fergus McCann and one who has remained shrouded in mystery over his Celtic connection – until now. Albert Friedberg, 45, is President of the Friedberg Mercantile Group, a major commodity, foreign-exchange and bond-trading group in Toronto. He was appointed by the Premier in Ontario to the Commodity Futures Advisory Board. McCann has spoken little about Friedberg – the man he described as his 'friend'. It is not known how long the two men have known each other. It is not known also what influence Friedberg can wield over Celtic's destiny. The Canadian money-man is also reluctant to talk about his financial involvement . . . as is Fergus McCann. What McCann has not revealed is that he is a *client* of Friedberg's.

Friedberg makes money. Lots of it. He is also into 'money management' and invests for himself and on behalf of his clients in many risky ventures. His Friedberg Mercantile Group began life in the commodities market where survival is a matter of guessing the right side of supply and demand.

He is also into discount-brokerage services and foreign-exchange dealing. Friedberg refuses to say why he chose to invest £1 million personally in Celtic and a further £1 million through an offshore firm he is involved in, or if that is his only financial stake now or in the future.

He has been to Glasgow only twice in connection with Celtic, and the last time was in the summer. From his plush home in North York near Toronto, he said: 'I know Fergus because he is a long-standing client but I would rather not get involved in any details. I am an investor in Celtic and was last over seeing them some time ago.

'The game was not significant. I was over to talk to Fergus. I follow the results and have an attachment to the game through my time in South America. I do not talk to Fergus very often.' As for additional investment in the club he added: 'These things depend on developments.'

Despite his stature in financial circles, Friedberg prefers to keep a low profile – much like McCann. But one story the Canadian media did follow with interest was when Friedberg 'donated' two art collections to the Royal Ontario Museum. He bought one, an Islamic textiles collection, for £33,000. Its value was put at almost £250,000 when it was transferred to the museum. The second collection was bought for £6,000 and transferred with a value of £115,000. Friedberg made a profit on the transaction because the tax savings he applied for were worth more than the total purchase price of the collections. The treasury took the matter to court but lost. However, on appeal, a judge ruled that one of the collections had not been purchased under Friedberg's name and, therefore, he could not claim the tax back.

The Financial Post, based in Toronto, is the biggest and most influencial financial newspaper on the east coast. Journalists there know of Friedberg but not one has ever heard of McCann. Writer Richard Blackwell said: 'If he is as big as people are making him out to be, we should have known about him. The bottom line is we do not. We only became aware of McCann after calls from journalists in Scotland. We have nothing on him on file for the period he spent here.'

TWO thousand miles away in Scottsdale, Arizona, it is the same story regarding McCann's anonimity. The little tourist town basking in the desert heat between Phoenix and the appropriately named Paradise Valley, is where McCann liked to spend the winter months away from the chill of Canada.

It is as close to the real cowboy country as anyone can get, as it is situated beside the Colorado River and the Grand Canyon and, like Montreal, is surrounded by Indian reservations.

In Scottsdale, McCann is not only virtually unheard of but practically unseen. His hideaway is a two-bedroom apartment which costs around £500 a month to rent. It is nestled in a maze of identical, whitewashed holiday-style flats with blue canopies in a complex appropriately named Sunscape Apartments.

Apart from the reception staff at his rented condominium, no one appeared to have seen or heard of the man McCann. The neighbours change frequently and no one appeared to remember a small bescpectacled Scotsman wandering about.

A receptionist who called herself Julie said: 'I only saw him at rent time and never saw him with anyone else. I guessed he was pretty rich but he was a very low-key person. It didn't seem as if anything bothered him.'

McCann's only link there with the outside world, and Celtic dealings in particular, was a telephone and fax machine. He spent much of the winter months plotting the downfall of the old Celtic board from his Scottsdale apartment. It was there that he received a call from Brian Dempsey telling him a collapse was imminent and suggesting he flew to Glasgow for talks.

But most of McCann's time in Arizona was spent playing golf in varying degrees of stifling heat. The 400-plus apartments at Sunscape are described in the brochure as 'keeping all the promises of a secluded paradise'.

The Mediterranean-style development has the advantage of backing on to an 'oasis-like golf course'. It allowed

McCann and the other residents the facility of walking a few hundred yards from their apartments straight on to the first tee at the Continental Golf Course. The course is an easy, low-par 60 with 12 of its 18 holes a par three. It is also a public course costing £16 a round, and the one preferred by McCann despite the option of around 80 others in the valley.

Reception staff at the complex could shed little light on their annual Scottish guest.

One said: 'I know who you're talking about, but I can't even remember talking to him or him talking to us apart from passing the time of day.'

Journalist Mark Scarp from the Scottsdale *Progress and Tribune* said: 'If you want to blend into the background then an apartment at the Sunscape development is the place to be. It is not expensive and is such a big development that a person can easily come and go almost unnoticed and without any contact with those around him.

'Certainly we have never heard of this guy and he is not known in any of the main golf circles around the town. He sounds a real mystery man.'

FERGUS McCann also has his own Bermuda triangle.

The Atlantic tax haven about 700 miles off the eastern coast of America is where McCann's business interests are registered.

Surrounded by the warm, blue waters of the Gulf Stream, it is a haven for divers, sailors and golfers with more golf courses per square mile than anywhere else in the world.

The British colony has one of the best climates in the world with the temperature often soaring above the 90s and seldom falling below 70. It is also a place of many millionaires and many secrets.

The tropical paradise island holds the key to many of the mysteries surrounding McCann . . . but it also throws up a few others.

In McCann's case there is the mystery of an official document amended to remove his name; the transfer of funds; and a man called Deuss.

The small capital town of Hamilton with its quaint pink, yellow and blue pastel buildings is the base for the company which was used to launch the shares option for Celtic: a company called Firstgreen Ltd. McCann described himself as President of Firstgreen, his investment and direct marketing firm. And he used the firm to front an advertisement in the Scottish press outlining his intentions for Celtic and seeking support.

The company was registered in Bermuda in March 1985 with a minimum capital of $12,000 US. It is an exempted company for tax purposes as it is an offshore business. Official paperwork relating to such companies registered in Bermuda is scarce. But even the few sheets relating to Firstgreen Ltd threw up one mystery.

The name of Fergus McCann does not appear on the documentation except for on one page where McCann's name has been blotted out. Tippex was used to cover over his name, and in his place appeared the name of Stephen P. Cook along with David G. Cooper and James F. Chapman. All British and all living in Bermuda. They were also three lawyers from the same firm on the island used by McCann.

Officials couldn't explain the cover-up at first, but later said McCann's name had been typed in 'by mistake' by his lawyers. At their offices in The Corner House, Hamilton, David Cooper said: 'You will find it is quite legal to have nominee shareholders and directors.' Asked about McCann he said: 'I met him a number of years ago when he acquired property in Bermuda.

'He is a pugnacious self-starter and a single-minded businessman. At one time he spent a lot of time in Bermuda but obviously is here less now.' The lawyer said he couldn't and wouldn't discuss his client's activities. In fact, he was rather annoyed with himself that he had spoken at all.

The property McCann bought in Bermuda is on a hillside overlooking the bay at Hamilton. It is within a complex of peach-coloured two-in-a-block flats on the outskirts of the town. The two-bedroom apartment is also one of the cheaper properties on the island and is completely dwarfed by the massive mansions that other millionaires live in. And, according to one of his neighbours, it is a place more enjoyable when McCann is *not* around.

A couple of his neighbours are not impressed with the small, balding Scotsman. One of them, Englishwoman Joan Darling, has lived in the complex for more than ten years. As she lazed at the poolside with another neighbour, the divorcee said: 'McCann? That small, obnoxious man? He is a mean, very rude bee. The first time I met him was when he came storming out at the back of the apartments insisting whoever had parked in his parking space remove their car immediately. He didn't even have a car here.

'Another time I was talking to a neighbour and he just barged into the conversation mumbling something. I don't even know what it was all about. We are all in such close proximity here that you want nice people around you.

'We all assumed he had some business here and was fairly well off, but he just wandered in and out and, thankfully, we don't see him very often.'

But the mystery is what McCann does with the flat when he is not there. McCann rents the apartment out. What is surprising is who he rents it to – John Deuss, one of the richest men to frequent the island. At 51, he is a billionaire.

Danish-born, he is owner of Transworld Oil, a major

international oil company. He has been involved in several deals which have been the subject of much discussion including one multi-million-pound project involving Russia, an Oman state oil company with which he was heavily involved, and oil giants Chevron. It is reported he wanted a hefty involvment from Chevron but little from Oman in a project to bring oil out of Russia to the West.

Deuss, through his company, rented McCann's apartment for around £2,000 a month, to house his personal pilot when he is on the island, despite owning three mansions in Bermuda. Around the same time, the great Dane had also bought a major stake in the Bermuda Commercial Bank of which he became chairman – a move regarded by many as securing even more confidentiality over his fortune and enabling easier dealings abroad.

It is not known what connection, if any, Deuss has directly with McCann, but Bermudan journalist Don Grearson believes the two men must know each other. He said: 'Deuss is the kind of guy you do not want to cross. He is very good to those loyal to him but can ruin those who turn against him. He also makes a lot of enemies. Deuss is not quite a recluse but he keeps very much in the shadows. For that reason he has everyone vetted thoroughly before he has any dealings with them. If he rents McCann's apartment then you can bet he knows him.' No one knows if there is any connection between Deuss, McCann and Montreal-based Albert Friedberg who manages some of McCann's financial affairs, but to many interested observers of Celtic they would not be in the least bit surprised if there were.

The mystery is not confined to Celtic supporters in Scotland. Bermudan police sergeant Charlie Mooney, president of the island's Celtic Supporters Club, added: 'We didn't know who McCann was, the fact he had property and came here or his Celtic connections until the takeover. We haven't seen him or spoken to him as he is seldom here.

'If he's coming over then I'm sure a few of the boys would enjoy a couple of drinks and a chat, although I'm not so sure McCann would like that.'

Word got back to McCann that his background was being looked into by a Scottish journalist. He didn't like that. And now he didn't like the journalist. Another one not to be trusted. And the list was growing.

THREE

Shinty

FOR Fergus McCann, making enemies was really easy and making friends was really hard. But there was one person he felt close to. A person he felt he could trust and one who seemed to understand him, support him even, and who had done so since his arrival in Scotland.

She was the blonde who had sat opposite him once as he battled with the other rebel leaders for control of the club months before.

Now she sat by his side and that comforted him. She was there to listen, to advise, but, ultimately, to obey, for that was what she was paid to do.

Her name was Elspeth Campbell, a corporate lawyer with Glasgow firm McGrigor Donald. The 32-year-old may have been more than twenty years younger than the Celtic supremo but the meetings between them quickly became more personal.

After only a few weeks at Celtic Park, the two joined football financial groupie David Low and his wife for a meal in Glasgow's West End.

Low, who had been paid to assist Dempsey and McCann in the run-up to the takeover, had been retained by McCann in a small consultancy capacity. It was Low who played Cupid and helped bridge the gap between business and pleasure for McCann and Campbell.

The pair struck up an unlikely partnership. Campbell was known as a bit of a socialiser while McCann preferred the quieter bachelor life. It was one partnership deal McCann hadn't banked on and, despite frequent dinners and stolen weekends, the relationship took a bit of a back seat as McCann pursued the next phase of his Celtic dream – a shares issue.

MCCANN'S plans to refinance the club through a major shares issue had been a long time in the planning.

As far back as 1990 – four years before control of the club was eventually won – McCann and the other rebels had already devised and drawn up a hefty 38-page prospectus to issue shares on behalf of a shadow company to assume control of Celtic.

The company was called 'Shinty's Future plc'. Shinty was their codename for Celtic and it seemed fitting. Shinty is a tough Scottish game and the battle for control of a football club like Celtic was as tough as it gets.

The game plan was for the leading investors from the rebel group to take 135,000 ordinary shares and 35,000 preference shares with a further 35,000 ordinary and 35,000 preference shares to be made available to the general supporters.

Such an injection of funds would contribute towards the rebuilding of Celtic Park with the then Cambuslang dream – the idea of building a new stadium there – well and truly dumped.

A draft letter written by McCann, intended for all Celtic fans, described Shinty's Future plc – which would be changed to Celtic's Future plc if the rebels were successful in taking control – as '. . . a new company formed with the objective of bringing together people who share the common purpose of raising funds for Shinty thereby helping to ensure its ability to survive and prosper as a leading Scottish Football club.'

McCann continued: 'For more than three years I have attempted to negotiate with the board of Shinty in order to get them to accept an investment in the club and to achieve the objectives outlined.

'These attempts were unsuccessful and my recent offer to meet with the board of Shinty has so far not been taken up. I feel that the club now has an urgent need for new funding, a fact that was recently accepted by the Shinty board.

'I have so far been unable to convince the Shinty board of the merits of our case. Accordingly, I have formed Shinty's Future in order to bring the matter into the public domain in the belief that the shareholders of Shinty will accept that the best interests of the club will be served by a substantial investment in it.'

Even at that stage, McCann insisted that he would have the lion's share with an investment of £7.2 million and individual control.

Brian Dempsey was not keen on that and he told McCann so. It was Dempsey's belief that no one individual should have overall control of the club and that a group of 'Celtic-minded people' should have overall say.

He suggested McCann reduce his personal stake by around 20 per cent. But McCann was having none of it.

In a letter to Dempsey in December 1990, McCann wrote: 'I will not make this investment and commitment – or anything similar – in order to be in a minority position – i.e. a total commitment or not at all.

'My exposure with £7 million in equity locked into a difficult business, plus five years in a tough job at a low salary, then a personal guarantee of a £5 million bank loan, ending with an obligation to sell at a price and date I cannot change, is more than you could expect from any investor. In other words, with the advantages in place for the lead investors, this deal is as good as you are going to find.

'To make anything happen, some risk has to be taken. For the investors, the downside is very good. But no one is going to double his money overnight.

'I broached the possibility of my offering a buy-out clause whereby the lead investors could take me out in the first three years if they agreed I was acting against the interest of the club. However, this "don't really trust him" option may not look good in the prospectus.

'At the end of the day it comes down to backing the horse you think has the best chance of winning – then cheering him on. Three things I am sure of: this deal is as good as it's ever going to get (for all concerned); the time is now as the opportunity is outstanding; there are few other Fergus McCanns likely to appear.'

McCann ended his letter by threatening to find other investors or to walk away. He wrote: 'I need letters of intent from your friends, otherwise we can then decide to approach other investors or, after 41 days running around Glasgow, I shall return to Montreal . . .'

McCann got his way and the plans were put in motion, although it was to take some time before 'Shinty' became a powerful reality.

The first attempt at an extraordinary general meeting of the club faltered.

The second bite came two years later in the autumn of 1993. Again it ended in failure, but the issue of the Cambuslang project and the funding for a new stadium to be built there had been well aired. That meeting was the last chance for the old board, and they knew it. But it was also the point where Dempsey suddenly realised that McCann would do anything to gain control. Anything.

At the meeting McCann claimed that even the consultants being used by Celtic were doubtful that the Cambuslang project would ever happen.

McCann said he had telephoned Superstadia and was adamant that the London-based consultants had told him they doubted the project.

Celtic director, David Smith, disagreed and claimed McCann was wrong. David Smith had a tape-recording of the telephone conversation which Superstadia had made.

But, before he could use that to his benefit, Smith was forced into a debate with Dempsey over club finances and the edge he held – and the tape – were history.

Dempsey recalled: 'I thought Fergus McCann was a man of immensely high principles when I first met him, only to realise that he was not. He deceived many people – me included – and he publicly misled us at that shareholders meeting .

'I'll never forget that night where he addressed David Smith about Superstadia and David Smith accused him of not being entirely truthful in public and said he had taped the conversation. Fergus and Charles Barnett (the rebels' PR guru) signalled me to get on my feet because of the situation, which I did. That was a terrifying moment for me because I have never lied to the public, the fans or the press. I have always been very careful publicly. Watching this happen filled me with terror – here was a man standing up to shareholders, the conversation had been taped, yet according to David Smith who was prepared to replay the tape to us all, he was prepared to be more than economical with the truth.

'McCann had phoned Superstadia to enquire about the real purpose of Cambuslang and how it would work. He recounted to the shareholders the fruits of that discussion. David Smith denied it and said he had a tape of the conversation and said that he wasn't lying.

'Superstadia had taped the conversation with Mr McCann and I had to stand up to deflect the conversation away from that issue. I didn't like that. I learned lots of things that night which frightened me. That was the start and ever since then we have seen everyone has been a liar. Everyone but Fergus McCann.'

A summary of the shares' prospectus of Shinty, which would have been put out if that night had been won, referred to the failure of the then board of directors as 'due to well-publicised internal disputes' and that they have 'not yet made public any coherent proposals to address the difficulties.

'Press coverage has estimated that it would cost £25 million to £40 million to redevelop the existing stadium or even more to resite it.

'It is our belief that the proposed investment of some £17 million, while not sufficient in itself to pay for the reconstruction of Shinty Park, would provide a sound base from which the club should be able to finance the necessary expenditure.'

It had taken six more months of fighting before the rebels had finally taken control and Shinty's Future had become Celtic's Future with McCann's investment firm, Firstgreen, having prepared the groundwork and tested the water as far as the support of the fans was concerned.

IT was in December 1994, a little over eight months since the take over, that the shares issue was finally launched.

There were those who doubted its success. With a minimum block of ten shares costing £620, many considered them beyond the pocket of the ordinary supporter – especially coming five days before Christmas.

McCann announced the move to the press saying the money would go to meet two crucial objectives: 'The strengthening of the football team in a major way, by providing money for new players, and also to part-finance the building of one of Europe's top football stadia.'

He continued: 'For the first time in their 106-year history, Celtic fans will be able to buy a stake in the club through the issue of new units at a price of £620 a unit, with each unit made up of ordinary and preference shares.'

The Co-operative Bank, the newly appointed banker to Celtic, said it would be offering cheap loans to fans wishing to take part in the offer. Supporters could borrow up to 80 per cent of the cost of the shares at a low rate.

McCann told the media: 'I am delighted that the ownership of Celtic will finally be available to a large number of supporters of the club.'

He added: 'The financing package will enable supporters to own part of Celtic for as little as £7.77 a week, which is less than the price of a match ticket. I urge Celtic fans everywhere to take up this opportunity, which is the first time in more than 100 years that Celtic ownership has been available to everyone. The opportunity may not arise for another 100 years – do not miss your opportunity to be a major player in putting Celtic back at the top of football.'

The shares being offered to the public through Glasgow stockbrokers Greig Middleton & Co Ltd would raise up to £5.4 million. The offer was also partially underwritten by lead investors.

It was interesting to note that the remaining shares were placed with Quay Financial Services (QFS) for a total consideration of £4 million.

QFS is part of the group owned by the Dublin millionaire Dermot Desmond, whose colourful and controversial background was yet to be unleashed on an unsuspecting Celtic support.

The subscription list for shares was to close on 24 January. Holders of each of the units were to be entitled to one vote at Celtic's AGM and the cash was to be used to achieve the prime objectives of rebuilding the Celtic team and redeveloping Celtic Park.

The prospectus – which had changed little from the first draft four years earlier – added: 'The football management team has identified specific sections of the first-team squad that need to be strengthened as a priority for Celtic to compete at the highest possible level in both national and international competitions.'

It said the directors fully supported the manager's approach and had told him of the 'significant funding' which would now be available to buy players. This would be supplemented by cash raised from the sale of players and would allow the manager to continue to rebuild the team.

It wasn't long before the media began asking who Dermot Desmond was and what his investment meant.

According to press reports at the time, Desmond's decision to buy £2 million worth of shares with a further interest in another £2 million was taken for commercial reasons. However, his aide, Ms Eileen Gleeson, revealed that Mr Desmond was also investing in Celtic because he was a supporter of the club. Mr Desmond, she said, had agreed to buy the shares himself and would be nominating a director to the board. That turned out to be himself.

At the same time Celtic all but severed its 106-year link with the Bank of Scotland when it announced that the Co-operative Bank was to be the club's new principal banker. McCann said: 'I want to thank the Bank of Scotland for its courtesies over the last several months. Unfortunately, the level of support required by Celtic was not obtainable from them at this time.'

The Bank of Scotland declined to comment. But many saw the move as McCann's way of dealing with a bank which had dealt quite severely with Celtic in the run-up to the takeover. It was also his aim to get rid of further 'old ties'.

Another old tie McCann was keen to get rid of once and for all was Brian Dempsey. But he needed him.

Both Dempsey and Gerald Weisfeld – the stores millionaire who had failed in an earlier bid to take control of Celtic – were important to McCann in his bid to have the new shares issue passed at a shareholders meeting.

He needed a united front, and that was exactly what was portrayed to the media. But the media were not completely fooled.

After the meeting on 19 April 1994, the *Herald* reported: 'Celtic's disparate power-brokers adopted a united front yesterday with the unanimous approval of a £21-million share issue for the beleaguered club. The issue was passed at an extraordinary general meeting yesterday, which also heard the ambitious plans to rebuild Celtic Park over the next two years at a cost of £24 million.'

The final composition of the Celtic board, however, still remained unclear, with key players Brian Dempsey and Gerald Weisfeld refusing to be drawn on their future role with the club. Club officials were anxious to stress that the meeting – which lasted just over an hour – had been a harmonious one and that Celtic were entering a new era of co-operation and conciliation. Both Mr Weisfeld and Mr Dempsey rallied publicly behind managing director Fergus McCann. Speaking after the meeting, Mr McCann said that under the share issue, shareholders had 14 days to take up their rights. For every two shares they held, they could buy 23 more Ordinary shares and 12 Preferential shares.

He said that in the next few months the club would go to the supporters with £5.4 million worth of shares and added that in the next two to three weeks 'the debt position of the club will be removed'. He said they were expecting to pay £24 million to rebuild Celtic Park. Asked if he had any announcements about changes to the Celtic board, Mr McCann said: 'The question of any board changes was not for today's meeting. We hope in the fullness of time we will have a strengthening from various areas. We hope to have representation from the supporters on the board. We expect to have an individual assigned to that side.' He added: 'A rather boring meeting, I'm afraid. No fights.'

Not at that point maybe, but there was plenty of in-fighting going on.

Dempsey, speaking to the press afterwards, played the game and would also not be drawn on whether he would take up a position on the Celtic board.

'The new shareholders will decide if they want to have additions to the Celtic board. In the very early days, Fergus offered me a position. I felt I was unable to accept it at that time.'

Asked if that invitation was still there, he said: 'I never regarded it as open. It's not important, it's not what this is all about. I have said to Fergus I will help in whatever way I can.' Asked to comment on rumours of a rift between himself and Mr McCann, he said their relationship was: 'As it has been since day one – enjoyable, healthy, constructive, not agreeing all the time, but it never should be. I hope it's filled with mutual respect. We share the same goal as to what we are trying to achieve.' If only Dempsey believed that.

Weisfeld was equally keen to stress the spirit of co-operation among the club's key players. He said: 'What's going to occur from now on is up to Fergus. He's the man in charge. We express a great deal of confidence in him. We could not ask for a better team and we are all going to give him our full backing. We have every reason to hope that the money will be spent in the right manner for the benefit of Celtic FC, and that it will enable the club to start performing to its potential.'

McCann sensed that everything was going according to plan. But, as he discovered, the media does not accept things at face value.

Within a few days *The Herald* ran another story casting doubts over McCann's figures.

It read:

> The rebuilding of Celtic Park still hangs in the balance, even if every new share offered to the public this week is snapped up by the club's supporters by the 24 January deadline.
>
> A detailed *Herald* investigation of Celtic's share-offer prospectus raises serious doubts about whether the club can really use the proceeds, as they claim, to support both the rebuilding of the team and the redevelopment of the park. Our investigation shows that if, as Fergus McCann, Celtic's chairman and managing director, has claimed, the 'lion's share' of the £8.9 million net proceeds is to be used to buy new players, Celtic could be forced to borrow an additional £20 million or more, if the three-quarters demolished Celtic Park is to be redeveloped to plan. Even to complete the first phase, the building of a new North Stand, seating 26,000, in time for the start of the 1995–96 season, could require Celtic to borrow up to £10 million, to finance its £16.9 million cost.
>
> McCann confirmed to *The Herald* that a 'substantial line of credit with the Co-operative Bank' has been established. He added that it's currently between £5 million and £10 million. However, McCann insisted that only a fraction of that facility would be needed by Celtic to complete phase one of the ground redevelopment programme.
>
> He added that the club had considered leasing some of the planned facilities, but decided bank finance and other resources would be a more economic option.

And there was more . . .

Celtic's prospectus reveals that, as late as last month, the club had cash balances of only £4.71 million and outstanding debts of £1.03 million. Of the £12 million raised in last May's rights issue (from McCann and the lead investors), £5.3 million was used to pay off the club's overdraft with their previous bankers, Bank of Scotland, and a further £2.65 million has been used to buy new players this season. There are many other calls on the club's existing resources. The prospectus reveals that Celtic is to pay £175,000 to the Inland Revenue in settlement of a PAYE investigation. A further liability of £130,000 is still in dispute.

An unsecured loan of £1 million made by Eddie Keane to Celtic earlier this month to buy players must be repaid next December. Celtic is committed to pay £450,000 under an operating lease for land and buildings, thought to be Hampden Park, this year, while its own ground is being rebuilt. There are also a number of outstanding claims against the club for which no provision has been made.

Even if the present share offer is fully subscribed and raises a net £8.9 million and if, as McCann has promised, the lion's share of that cash goes on new players, Celtic will still be well adrift of the funds needed to redevelop Celtic Park.

The Celtic prospectus states that the £16.9 million cost of completing the North Stand will be financed 'from current cash resources, available bank, and other loan facilities, Football Trust grants, and the minimum subscription'. The minimum subscription was the £8.2 million, less expenses, due to be raised from the underwritten and placed elements of the current share offer. A £4 million package of shares has been pre-placed with QFS Financial Services of Dublin, in which Dermot Desmond has an interest, but only if the other directors matched it. The £4 million worth of the shares match were underwritten, £2.5 million of them by two Celtic directors, Willie Haughey and John Keane, and by Gerald Weisfeld and Eddie Keane. Only £500,000 would come from McCann. However, McCann has already said that the bulk of that money will go on players, although Celtic sources are now playing down speculation on the sports pages that manager Tommy Burns will have between £7 million and £8 million to spend.

The seeds of doubt were now very firmly in place. McCann's sums didn't add up, and only time would tell whether the stadium or the team would benefit from the cash.

WILLIE Haughey had taken up a seat on the board six months after the takeover. The millionaire city business-man had already tried and failed, along with Gerald Weisfeld, to buy out the old board. They ran head to head with McCann and Dempsey in the battle for control.

In the early days, after the rebels had won, Haughey and Weisfeld were paraded as part of the 'green dream team' but there was no immediate inclusion on the board for them.

A long, slow process of getting the two sides together had been happening behind the scenes.

Only a few days after the takeover at Celtic Park, Dempsey said he was hopeful that Weisfeld could be encouraged to invest in the Parkhead club, and he urged the two to avoid what he called 'a battle of egos or conflict of personalities'. He said at the time: 'I think that Fergus McCann needs to get as many facts together as he can so that he can have a productive discussion with Gerald Weisfeld, and I earnestly hope that we can have a marriage of ideas, expertise and funding. Their first task will be to get to know and trust each other. These are two highly successful individuals who have been used to running their own empires.'

Later, Weisfeld refused to discuss his intentions but indicated that he was willing to inject some of the millions of pounds he made from the What Everyone Wants chain of shops into Celtic, adding that he had 'some ideas for the club'.

His ideas, though, would be fed into the club many months later through his stepson Michael McDonald, for both Weisfeld and Dempsey knew that the clash of egos had already happened.

During the takeover Dempsey had suggested that McCann meet Wiesfeld with a view to them both being involved in the new Celtic.

The meeting was arranged at a lawyer's office in Glasgow.

McCann arrived early with Dempsey and took up his position on a seat at the head of a long boardroom table.

Weisfeld arrived through the door at the other end of the room. McCann didn't even raise his head from some paperwork he was reading. He stayed seated and waited for Weisfeld to come across the room to him. It was first-class one-upmanship.

After Dempsey introduced them, McCann quickly, and with few words, made it clear that there would be only one man in control at Celtic, and that man was him.

Weisfeld retained his composure, told McCann he saw no reason to play second fiddle to him, thanked him for his time and walked out.

The meeting had lasted only a few minutes.

Six months after the takeover, when Weisfeld did invest, it was Michael McDonald who took his seat on the board.

He had Haughey for support and Dominic Keane who had helped the Weisfeld camp in their earlier bid for control.

To this day Keane believes that, if the two opposing factions had got together earlier, the rescue of Celtic and the way it was then run would have been different.

Keane recalled: 'In the days leading up to the takeover we had the support of two directors, Kevin Kelly and Tom Grant. And it is fair to say that I think the reason they came to us wasn't because of Fergus McCann, it was because they trusted people like John Keane, Brian Dempsey and me.

'They knew of our association with Willie Haughey and Gerry Weisfeld, although there were still two camps at that time. I think one of the tragedies was that the Willie and Gerald group didn't get closer to Brian, John Keane and me. Although the history books will show they probably did come together after the event, I think it's a tragedy that they couldn't have got together earlier which would have made more for a solid board then.

'I think that would have meant that the distribution of the shares would have been more equal. One of the things that Fergus was looking for was delegated responsibility to get on with doing the job, and, to be fair, that was one of the things he got from the new board. But there's delegated responsibility and there's delegated responsibility. At first we were consulted on a whole range of issues but as McCann became stronger and closer to an issue then it was clear that more and more things were being kept in the background. He was taking control and the rest of us were being kept in the dark.'

Haughey also remembers those early dealings and how the situation could have been very different – even to the extent that Brian Dempsey could have become chairman if he had chosen the right camp.

Haughey said: 'I was involved early on when I bought 40 shares from a gentleman down in Wales, and years ago you couldn't buy the shares just like that, so I had to go to a couple of the AGMs by proxy vote. That was at the time when Brian and Fergus were making a play to takeover the club.

'I went to AGMs and I wasn't happy the way things were going with the board not wanting to accept others investing. I thought the first time around it was a big opportunity missed when Fergus went away with his £8.5 million as there weren't that many people about wanting to put that sort of money in football. Then one day I offered to buy out the board – who had a 60 per cent stake in the company between them and through Dave Smith I had that agreement; so much so that I had lodged the money in the bank, £3.6 million. But the one thing I would not accept was that any of the old board members remained.

'Michael Kelly and Dave Smith and Chris Whyte were quite happy with that, but Kevin Kelly and Tom Grant weren't. So I spoke to Gerry Weisfeld and got his support. I saw Jack McGinn and Jim Farrell as not being part of the pack, so I was happy to keep them on board.

'Early on in the proceedings, when the press started to try and promote the idea of rival factions, I approached Dominic Keane after my very first meeting with Dave Smith. I also phoned Brian Dempsey and the very next day I met him in Jimmy Farrell's office.

'I told him that the old board would not sell to Brian or Fergus but it was a possibility they would sell to me. I told them that they could not preclude me from going and making a deal with anybody if I chose to.

'I was up front and I was telling him I could go into the old board and do a deal and then could walk into another room and do a deal with Fergus and we would walk out to meet the press together.

'All the way through I kept Brian and Dominic informed of all my discussions and all my dealings. We were offering £300 a share and most of them were ready to take it. But I'm not sure if Brian Dempsey told the other Scottish investors about my offer.

'In the end, when the final moves were being made, Dominic told me that Michael Kelly was the one holding out for more money and that he was trying to do a deal with him.

'When Dominic came out and said he had done the deal then Fergus took over. Fergus and his side managed to secure the other shares. It seemed we weren't part of it then. Me, Gerry and Michael made noises about being interested and wanted to see if there was anything we could offer the party. I had about a 45-minute meeting with Fergus and he told me that any Celtic people who were business-minded he would listen to, and he did just that.

If we wanted to participate in the share, they'd like us – me, Michael and John Keane – to join the board. Fergus took over in March and Michael and John and I went in in September.'

Dempsey lost out and had now decided to walk away. McCann believed everything was working out as it should, although he still had his problems and there was a long, long way to go.

Speaking at the time, he said: 'This whole idea of me being a workaholic and a one-man team is nonsense. We will soon have six executives with important duties working here.'

But he admitted: 'Every day I say to myself: "Why am I blowing my brains out?" There are crises every day, people wanting immediate answers and instant results. The hardest part of this job will be to make progress on all fronts and, above all else, we have to put a strong team on the field.

'At least we can say that all the negative vibes that were around the dressing-room before the changes have now been removed and team spirit has been restored. Everybody here feels that the dismissal of Lou Macari was a positive, not a negative, move.

'We also have to provide a good stadium for the supporters and we have to end the "cut back" mentality that existed here because there was no money.'

Although his words may have come back to haunt him, as far as McCann was concerned, everything was now in place: a new board, a shares' prospectus and a new manager – Tommy Burns. And therein lay another dark chapter in Celtic's new history.

FOUR

Cloak and Dagger

GETTING rid of manager Lou Macari was one of McCann's first priorities. Finding a replacement was the next – when the new Celtic owner wasn't too busy with the shares prospectus.

Macari was rather unceremoniously booted out of Celtic Park in June 1994, three months after the takeover. McCann believed Macari was not committed to the job as he had refused to move permanently to Scotland, preferring to commute between his home in Stoke – where his wife and family remained – and Celtic Park.

It became yet another early mess splattered all over the press. But it was nothing compared to what was to come.

McCann made it known from the start that the man he wanted for the job was former Celtic idol Tommy Burns. The problem was that Burns and his assistant Billy Stark had two years left of a contract as management team at Kilmarnock.

What followed was to become one of the most astonishing 'poaching' sagas ever witnessed in Scottish football. It was to be filled with truths, half-truths and downright lies.

Within a couple of weeks of Macari's departure, Burns was in the frame. It took another week before McCann admitted it.

In a prepared statement, the Parkhead supremo said: 'There has been much speculation regarding candidates or even appointees for the position. I wish to make clear that none of these reports has any substance. But I want to make our position clear regarding Tommy Burns, presently player–manager at Kilmarnock Football Club.'

McCann said he had contacted Kilmarnock Chairman Bob Fleeting, who wanted to speak firstly to Burns, before replying. McCann added: 'I want to make it clear that we see Tommy Burns as a first-rate candidate for the position. And if he is able to obtain permission from his club to advance his career, I do wish to have a serious discussion with him regarding the position.'

Kilmarnock did not want to give that permission, but that didn't stop McCann. Burns was on holiday in Tenerife in the Canary Islands when he got a call saying McCann wanted to meet with him.

There then followed a cloak-and-dagger operation which McCann himself instigated and was involved in. Just over a week later on Monday, 11 July, Burns quit Kilmarnock under a cloud of anger and resentment. The accusations of poaching and tapping were flying everywhere.

The next day Burns was paraded by McCann at Celtic Park as the new manager there – described in most reports as 'Scottish football's worst-kept secret'.

Burns promised the fans: 'I'll put the heart back into Celtic!' The new boss was given a three-year contract and his prime target in his new £150,000-a-year post was to restore the spirit he had known during in his 15 years as a player with the club.

Burns declared: 'There is a passion about this club and a pride in playing for it and trying to win every game that seems to have disappeared, especially last season. I don't think I've got all the answers – but I do know what's right for Celtic. I can honestly say I've got their best interests at heart and I'll give this job everything I've got.'

McCann wasn't about to give anything, particularly to Kilmarnock, who were now baying for the blood of the Celtic managing director and threatening court action.

He underlined to the media that he had no intention of paying Kilmarnock any compensation saying: 'I don't see any reason why there should be compensation. If a person applies for a position then that is his affair and anything that follows as a result is between his former employer and himself. It's unfortunate for Tommy and Kilmarnock that this has happened, but Tommy gave them very good service for a number of years.'

McCann was to prove to have been more than a little economical with the truth when making those comments and others which were to follow. He insisted at the time that Celtic's legal advisers had told them there would be no comeback from the Scottish League over the Burns affair even though the former Rugby Park player and boss was still registered to play for Kilmarnock.

McCann said: 'Tommy has resigned from that post and he is retiring as a player and Celtic have no intention of registering him as a player.'

Burns added: 'The last 24 hours have been dreadful for me – but so have the last ten days. I had to do what I thought was best for me and sometimes that's a hard thing to do.'

Burns also blasted the sceptics who claimed he was too inexperienced to manage Celtic, adding: 'Some people can accumulate more experience in two years than others can do in ten. However, I know I've got a lot to do. Rangers have won everything going for the last six years and Celtic have won nothing. I'm not putting pressure on myself because I know that I have to get the club right before we can even approach them.'

Significantly, McCann refused to reveal just how much money Burns would be given to spend on new players, although he insisted that cash was there.

The following day Billy Stark quit Kilmarnock to join Burns at Celtic, further deepening the huge rift between the clubs.

It was fast becoming clear that, contrary to what McCann and his 'legal advisers' would have people believe, football bosses at both the SFA and the League were about to get involved.

Kilmarnock's anger over the affair was underlined by their reaction to Stark's decision.

A club statement insisted his resignation had not been accepted, adding: 'The matter has been reported to the Scottish League and SFA and we will be seeking compensation for the loss of Billy Stark as player and assistant manager.'

Celtic, and McCann's, arrogance over the issue remained. Club spokesman Peter McLean said: 'Our position remains the same, that Celtic have conducted their business in a correct fashion.' McLean refused to comment on claims from Kilmarnock that McCann had tapped Burns while he was under contract.

Scottish League secretary, Peter Donald, confirmed that a formal complaint had been received from the Rugby Park club and he indicated that Celtic 'would have some talking to do'.

He added: 'Kilmarnock's letter details circumstances which they believe put Celtic in breach of Scottish League rules and we will examine their claims and take the matter up with Celtic.'

That move convinced Kilmarnock to drop a legal action against Burns and Stark which was due to be called at the Court of Session in Edinburgh the following day.

Solicitors acting for Kilmarnock telephoned court officials instructing them to withdraw the action shortly before the 2 p.m. hearing was scheduled to begin.

Five weeks later McCann and Celtic were reeling from a massive £100,000 fine imposed on the club by the Scottish Football League.

The fine, the biggest ever in Scotland, was for enticing manager Burns away from Kilmarnock. The Scottish League found the club guilty of a breach of its rules governing approaches to players and managers under contract to other clubs. McCann was furious. He said: 'We feel that the decision is wrong and the fine excessive. We are likely to appeal, but we are also considering other options.'

The League also passed the papers concerning the case to the overall body, the SFA, which has wider powers and could impose another large sum as compensation to be paid to Kilmarnock. Kilmarnock chairman Bob Fleeting said: 'We get no satisfaction out of seeing a club fined. We decided to step back from court action in order to let Scottish football authorities deal with the matter. Now we must wait for the SFA's decisions before we decide what next. But personally I wish the whole business had never happened.'

The press had a field day. McCann had been well and truly rapped. Writing in the *Evening Times*, Alan Davidson summed it up:

> Fergus McCann has a lot of learning to do if he is to oversee the mighty task of turning Celtic around and re-establishing them as the major force they should be.
>
> Celtic, and McCann in particular, should be having a right good look in the mirror and asking questions of their own naïvety. Why McCann felt it necessary to personally sound out Burns beggars belief. Once it was discovered, and openly admitted to, what did he expect the Scottish League's interpretation of that little get-together to

be? A cosy chat over the price of a pint? The formation of a chapter of the Scottish–Canadian Friendship Society?

McCann's rescue package for the club was bold and hugely welcome, but since having kept the bailiffs from the door at Parkhead, his track record has scarcely been impressive. He must recognise the rules of the game were not established to be so blatantly disregarded by a man who knows virtually nothing of the structure of Scottish football.

It was an early and humiliating defeat for McCann and an equally early indication of how he chose to rule at Celtic.

And so the Burns saga continued. Kilmarnock threatened legal action again, this time against Celtic, looking for compensation.

Kilmarnock chairman Fleeting kept the pressure on McCann saying: 'It is an obligation on my part to get compensation for the club and its supporters, and if I were not to pursue it vigorously then I should not be here as chairman.'

McCann stubbornly reiterated his belief that he and his club had acted properly. He said Burns had applied for the position and Celtic had made the proper efforts to communicate with Kilmarnock.

McCann had a slight breather from the affair with the August financial figures announced. There were problems there, but he appeared to be happy that the club was looking a lot healthier. The redevelopment of Celtic Park was well under way and more finance for it would come from the new shares' issue.

Another deflection came with the news that Celtic were to sue former manager Lou Macari – who was raising a counter-case against the club seeking compensation over his sacking.

But Kilmarnock would not go away. By October the SFA had still not received word from Celtic as to whether they were going ahead with their final appeal against the £100,000 fine imposed on them by the Scottish League.

McCann refused to comment one way or the other, thus helping to confuse matters even more. Celtic had been decisively overruled by a special general meeting called by the club in protest against the League's decision and their objection to the size of the fine.

After a full three weeks of silence, the headlines appeared with McCann admitting defeat.

MCCANN PAYS FINE AND OPENS TALKS WITH KILMARNOCK was a typical headline in the papers that day. So, after weeks of appealing and posturing Celtic finally adopted what some writers described as 'a more acceptable attitude'.

Celtic's cheque for £100,000 arrived at the offices of the Scottish League and then the club revealed they had opened negotiations with Kilmarnock 'to resolve amicably'.

Two weeks later the SFA fined Burns and Stark £2,000 for breach of their contracts as players with the Ayrshire team and suspended them from playing any football. The SFA also gave both clubs 21 days to sort out their compensation row or the SFA would do it for them. The implication in the statement by SFA chief executive Jim Farry was clear: if the matter was not resolved by 7 December, Burns and Stark would be prevented from carrying on as managers of Celtic.

After lengthy deliberations at the SFA's Park Gardens HQ, it was pointed out that 'new evidence' in the case of Burns had come to light and the SFA intended acting upon it. McCann knew that settling the differences with Kilmarnock could lead to a more lenient view regarding the new evidence which the authorities considered serious.

It was also suggested to McCann that it would be a good idea to end the matter quickly as the team prepared for the Coca-Cola Cup final against Raith Rovers on Sunday, 27

November. It would be better for Burns and Stark to approach that match with nothing else on their minds.

But it was not to be. McCann would not pay what Kilmarnock demanded and the matter was then referred to a tribunal. It would be five months later before Celtic were ordered to stump up £200,000.

McCANN and Burns both know exactly what went on behind the scenes during those turbulent times. But there was one other who was party to it all. A man Tommy Burns had trusted for most of his football life, Frank Cairney, former general secretary of the Celtic Boys' Club.

Frank had spent some time in the shadows after leaving Celtic under a cloud in the early 1990s amid rumours involving the boys on a trip abroad.

He and another Boys' Club official, Jim Torbett, were later taken to court and faced allegations of sexual assault. Torbett was found guilty and jailed but the case against Cairney was thrown out.

He emerged completely vindicated, but his association with Celtic had suffered. McCann didn't want him on the scene, and he told Burns just that after seeing the manager pose for pictures with Cairney soon after taking up his post.

But McCann knew Cairney a lot better than people thought at the time. Cairney had been involved in the negotiations as McCann tried to persuade Burns to quit Kilmarnock and become Celtic manager.

Frank Cairney's version of events backs that of Tommy Burns in his claims over the Kilmarnock saga.

Cairney recalls it all very clearly. He said: 'I got involved on day one but I want to make clear what my role was. I never offered Tommy Burns the job on behalf of anyone and I didn't lobby him to take it. I got involved because of my friendship with him and his family.

'Tommy was in Tenerife on holiday with his family. I got a telephone call from him while he was out there. He had been contacted by Tommy Craig saying Fergus McCann wanted to see him. It was pretty obvious what Fergus was up to as there had been a delay in appointing a manager after Lou Macari was sacked.

'Tommy asked my advice and I suggested he meet the guy because he was having trouble finding a manager. Tommy then called Fergus from his hotel in Tenerife. He was still manager at Kilmarnock but he wanted to speak to Fergus.

'Fergus told Tommy he wanted him to fly back to Glasgow right then and to meet him at Glasgow airport. Tommy wasn't that daft. He said no to Glasgow because there was nowhere to hide and someone would have seen them. It was pretty naïve of McCann to have suggested that.

'Tommy suggested either Manchester or London. Fergus agreed to Manchester and Tommy called me back to tell me and asked me to help arrange the meeting.

'I booked Tommy and me into the Staneylands Hotel in Wilmslow and told him I would pick him up at the airport. I suggested he tell Fergus to book in somewhere else or just travel down for the day.

'Tommy called Fergus back and told him to meet us at the hotel but not to book into the same place. He also told him that I was arranging things. I then got a call from McCann's secretary, Kay Donachy, to ask me what was my involvement with this. I told her it was none of her business. She said Fergus wanted to know if I was acting as Tommy's agent. I said no, I was just helping him as a friend.

'I hired a car and drove to Manchester airport to meet

Tommy but we missed each other. There were two international terminals and I went to one while Tommy came through the other. Normally we would have found each other, but circumstances didn't allow that.

'Tommy was hoping not to be spotted by anyone and you would have expected him to get through the airport without being recognised. But not that day. He bumped into Brian McClair who asked him what he was doing in Manchester.

'Tommy made the excuse that he was down to watch a player at Barnsley. So he didn't hang about and took a taxi straight to the hotel.

'I eventually met up with him back there. Then came the shock when we discovered Fergus McCann had booked into the same hotel despite us telling him it would be more discreet if he was staying elsewhere.

'But it was too late to worry about that and, fortunately, no one there recognised either Tommy or Fergus.

'Tommy went off for a walk around the hotel grounds with Fergus. They spent about two, or even three, hours talking. McCann had sounded him out about the job and asked him if he was interested. It was now 10 p.m. on the Friday and Tommy said he wanted to have something to eat and to think things over.

'Tommy went to great lengths to tell Fergus that he was interested in the job, but he said the meeting they were having was completely off the record as he was still manager at Kilmarnock. He said he would only talk officially to Fergus if Fergus got permission from Kilmarnock to do so.

'Unfortunately, the Kilmarnock chairman Bob Fleeting was in America, so Tommy was charged with getting hold of the telephone number over there so that Fergus could talk with Bob Fleeting direct.

'The next morning Fergus asked Tommy about me and my role there. Tommy told him I was just a good friend who had done a lot for Celtic over the years. Then I joined the two of them for breakfast. Fergus was flying back to Glasgow that day and, in the summing up at the breakfast table, he asked where things now stood.

'Tommy said he would have to fly back to Tenerife because he had left his wife and children there. Fergus suggested to Tommy that it may not be worth while going back to Tenerife just then.

'But Tommy said there was no way he could go back to Glasgow when he was supposed to be on holiday. We reached a compromise and Tommy decided to come back and stay at my house in Uddingston and that was provisionally agreed before Fergus left.

'But things then started to get a bit messy. Tommy eventually got a number for Bob Fleeting without alerting anyone at the club to what was going on. He called Fergus who was now back in Glasgow that afternoon and gave him the number.

'Tommy asked Fergus what he was planning to do. After all, Tommy had to decide whether to spend hundreds of pounds trying to get back to Tenerife or whether it was worth his while going through all of that if Fergus was going to offer him the job. Fergus said that he planned to offer him the job, Tommy came back with me and spent three nights at my place.

'Fergus got a very sharp rejection from Bob Fleeting after the first call and it was then bartered about with frequent calls to me at home. Fergus was on the phone on Saturday, Sunday and Monday, day and night, to my place. But Tommy wouldn't have any official talks with Fergus until he got Kilmarnock's permission.

'On the Sunday, Tommy didn't want to miss mass as he usually goes to church, so we tried to disguise him a bit with a baseball cap pulled over his face. We went to St Columba's in Viewpark near my home. We almost got away with that completely but some of the altar boys recognised him. Fortunately no one else did and nothing came of it.

'All this time Tommy was calling Fleeting and the club secretary and trying to make out he was still in Tenerife. They were refusing point-blank to let him speak to Fergus officially. He was being blocked all along the road. They told Tommy that if he went to Celtic then they would put him out the game as he and Billy Stark were still registered as players with them.

'At one point, Tommy was just going to abandon the whole thing, but he then had a couple of meetings with Fergus. The first was in my office at night. I picked Fergus up from Celtic Park and drove him out. The meeting lasted about two and a half hours and then I took Fergus back to his flat in Glasgow.

'On the next Saturday, a week after the first hotel meeting, another meeting was arranged at a place in Glasgow city centre in West George Street. I think Fergus had called it Barclay's or something like that. We were late getting there because we couldn't find it. We thought Barclay's was the name of a pub beside the office, but it was actually Barkers, a PR firm used by Fergus.

'I was locked out of that meeting. Tommy then came out and said he'd been hounding Fergus to talk to Kilmarnock. He had also asked Fergus to talk to me about the Kilmarnock situation. Fergus came out the office with his bunnet on and a set of keys in his hand which he used to lock the office door.

'He got into the back of my car with Tommy in the front, and I was driving. I asked him where he was going. He said he was just going to Buchanan Street. It was pouring down outside and the car was steaming up which was okay as it meant no one was likely to recognise Tommy or Fergus.

'I drove off and said to Fergus: "You'll have to talk to Kilmarnock about compensation." He moaned and said they'd probably ask for half a million pounds. I suggested a buy-out of Tommy's contract – which was about £80,000 over the two years left. That's about all Tommy was getting at the time. But Fergus believed Kilmarnock would rip him off.

'I told him he would be bound by the same rules as Kilmarnock and the members of the same association, and that his relationship with other clubs was important as one day he might need the support of clubs like Kilmarnock.

'Tommy was on the verge of just walking away again.

'The next step was a meeting requested by Bob Fleeting. Tommy wanted to meet all the Kilmarnock directors, but Fleeting said he wanted to meet Tommy first. They arranged to see him at the Fenwick Hotel. But all Fleeting did was threaten to put Tommy out of the game.

'Tommy then went to a full meeting of the board. Most were sympathetic, but Tommy left the meeting in a bit of a state. He asked his wife, Rosemary, to call me and tell me he wasn't taking the Celtic job. He said it wasn't worth all the hassle.

'I called him and told him he would never get the chance of the Celtic job ever again. That's when he decided he would take it and said he would issue a press statement. Then he met Fergus in a Glasgow restaurant and agreed to a press conference at Celtic Park where they would say he was taking the job even though they were still in dispute with Kilmarnock.

'Despite what McCann said about Tommy soliciting the job from him, the truth is as I have stated. McCann knows that and so does Tommy.

'Fergus had even given Tommy a list of all the salaries being paid to those at Celtic Park in an effort to agree a wage with him. Tommy wasn't greedy and asked for something between Liam Brady's and Lou Macari's.'

The salary agreed was around £110,000. Cairney recalled how the problems didn't end there.

He added: 'Tommy had been in the job only a week when he became very bitter. As soon as Fergus got Tommy on board he treated him like a wee boy. Fergus had refused to agree compensation with Kilmarnock and had to go to a tribunal. It was held at a hotel in Cumbernauld and Fergus said Tommy had solicited the job from him. Tommy couldn't take it any more and said he was going in there to tell the truth. McCann was asked twice at the tribunal if he had approached Tommy and offered him the job. Twice he replied "No".

'Tommy went in and the chairman, a Lord somebody, asked him the same question and Tommy said "Yes". The chairman threw his pencil in the air and shrugged his shoulders.

'When they got back to Celtic Park Fergus was furious. He called all the directors into the room and said he wanted to sack Tommy. That was just two weeks before the Cup final.

'Tommy wanted to offer me some sort of job at Celtic but I said no to that. I was very close to Jock Stein but things had changed so much at Celtic since his days there. It's a pity he wasn't still around because he would have handled Fergus.'

But, back in November 1994, Tommy Burns was the manager and he was facing up to the Cup final – and the disaster Celtic didn't want to happen. Burns led his team into the Coca-Cola Cup final as the Kilmarnock dispute dragged on. First division Raith Rovers produced one of the biggest upsets in Scottish football to dump Celtic and lift the silverware. The sides had drawn 2–2 after extra time before Celtic lost on penalties. Instead of ending Celtic's five-year trophy famine, Tommy Burn's side left dejected, many in tears. And there would be plenty more tears to shed.

FIVE

Save Our Shares

DEFEAT was never easy for Fergus McCann to swallow. Defeat off the field was harder for him to bear than defeat on it. Although, it must be said, that victory for the team was crucial to him after the Cup defeat.

He was still in his first year at Celtic and the shares' issue was about to be launched. The timing really couldn't have been much worse. The Kilmarnock claim for compensation for tapping Burns had taken up a lot of his time. It was now becoming a thorn in his flesh, but McCann believed he could hold out and save money. He was to be proved wrong on that count.

He was also still on the wrong end of a bashing from the supporters over a 'fat cat' ticket offer – another money-making idea which had backfired.

Celtic had launched a scheme to milk even more money out of the hard-pressed fans by giving those who could afford it the chance to buy their way to a much-prized ticket for an Old Firm game at Ibrox.

Celtic only received 7,500 tickets for the game against Rangers, and Celtic season-ticket-holders faced a ballot for the much sought-after briefs. Then, out of the blue, came a meal ticket to the game for McCann. If the fans, who had already paid around £300 for a season-ticket, wanted to jump the ballot queue, all they had to do was stump up another £85 to have lunch at Celtic Park and then be bussed to Ibrox for the game.

It was about as popular as the plan for far-away fans to get a ticket for the Old Firm match at the New Year – another ticket offer for a match package to be bought up-front costing £95. Leaders of Celtic's Irish supporters' clubs refused to back the offer because of the upset it would cause to the Glasgow supporters. McCann dumped the idea.

This time around three hundred Old Firm tickets were held back until the club could gauge the response to the latest deal. But angry fans' leader, Peter Rafferty of the Affiliation of Registered Celtic Supporters' Clubs, blasted the move claiming it would alienate supporters.

He said: 'We are trying to avoid a two-tier system of those who have and those who have not. Now we see an offer being made to Celtic fans who have money and which undermines the fairness of the ballot.'

Celtic spokesman Peter McLean tried to defuse the situation by claiming: 'It is a special commercial promotion to try and build in additional incentives for season-ticket holders and we would certainly hope we would not alienate anyone. We would be interested to receive feedback on whether it is a popular offer or not.'

He got his answer rather quicker than he expected with one fan claiming: 'This is just sheer money-grabbing by McCann, which does nothing but upset the faithful sup-porters.'

All the problems would not help sell the shares McCann now planned to issue. The fans were clamouring for improvement on the park and not off it. Celtic were now playing their home games at Hampden Park while rebuilding work progressed, and the national stadium was anything but a home from home.

As Alan Davidson of the *Evening Times* put it:

This is a club which was at death's door less than a

year ago. It was expected to improve after a period of convalescence. It has now had a relapse. In a perfect world Hampden would be full for no other reason than that true fans would wish to chant the name of Paul McStay and give one of the club's players some heartfelt comfort. But it's not. Celtic fans, baffled and bewildered, are asking: 'Where do we go from here?' In all honesty – and with sincere sympathy – I just don't know. Celtic's crying need is obvious. But how they find a better class of player to support McStay, Boyd, Collins and O'Donnell is not at all clear. It makes no sense to sell the best players to fund replacements who will be no better and quite possibly worse. There would be no point in paying for a new roof on Glasgow's Art Gallery by flogging the Rembrandts inside it. Somehow, Fergus McCann must find money to give Tommy Burns a chance to strengthen the side so that it might, just might, become the second best in the country.

By then the friction between McCann and Burns was beginning to surface outside Celtic Park. It seemed Burns was expected to carry on trying to build a winning team with little or no money to spend on players.

McCann then spoke. He said that a way would be found to finance Tommy Burns's desire to improve the team. His first priority was to rebuild Celtic Park, but even he admitted he had become aware of the unrest among the support. He had heard the clamour drifting up from outside and he knew the majority of the supporters would be happy to sit in less luxurious surroundings just so long as money saved was spent on improving the team.

Tommy Burns was to recall those early months – and the bitterness which would quickly build up between him and McCann.

Burns said: 'Initially it was very difficult for us. We were both under a great deal of pressure to turn the club round and get things up and running. But there were so many confrontations in the early weeks that, basically, we drifted apart.'

He recalled how problems arose almost immediately over the buying and selling of players, adding: 'There were times when I wanted to sell a player the club didn't need but Mr McCann disagreed, and there was the occasion when I wanted to sign a player but it took weeks for Mr McCann to get back to me on it.

'I needed to buy and sell players quickly, but Mr McCann was always searching for a logic within that. Unfortunately, within football there is very little logic. When you're a manager and you want to get a player, you want to go and get him immediately.

'He wanted to negotiate the best deal for the club. I didn't have any problems with that, but he had to understand the speed with which it had to be done. He wanted to do it in his own time and, some of the time, he wasn't prepared to furnish me with the facts about exactly what was going on.

'Mr McCann wasn't a football person. He didn't understand the psychology of the game. He didn't like the emotion, the passion and the competitiveness attached to the game, anything like that. Basically, that's what keeps the game going.'

Back then, as Tommy Burns was to discover, the man was not for changing. McCann had a five-year plan and he was sticking to it.

Even though McCann had told journalists during the first year when the problems were surfacing: 'I will be trying to accelerate the release of finance to the manager and I believe I can find a way to meet his objectives. Although I'm sure Tommy Burns can be helped, the club will not be diverted from the task of rebuilding the stadium. We won't be splashing out on a star player just to make things look good.

'The long-term and short-term needs have to be addressed. I have had talks with Tommy over the past couple of days, and there would be little point in altering the overall plan at this stage.'

While accepting that defeat by Raith Rovers was deeply disappointing, McCann claimed it was not a crisis and that he had encouraging feedback from supporters who wanted to help take the club forward. That appeared to be a reference to those people whom he hoped would take up the opportunity to buy shares in the club, which McCann hoped would bring in a substantial amount of money.

There was a growing army of those who doubted if the shares issue would be successful. Fans were being asked to fork out a minimum of £600 for a block of ten shares when money was tight and morale was low.

McCann added: 'We are trying to get a package to suit everyone, and the offer will have to have four things. First, it has to benefit the club, the playing side and also the operational side. Second, it has to give a voting say and ownership rights. Third, it has to be an investment which is reasonably priced and with a reasonable growth. Fourth, there must be benefits which suit the shareholders.'

He then added his own little quip: 'People won't be asked to pay the £300 a share which I paid to get some people out of the way.'

But even with low-interest loans being made available to help make it possible for as many of the ordinary fans as possible to invest, the doubts were still there. It was, indeed, a crucial period for Celtic and for McCann in particular. His five-year plan could succeed or fail on the result.

THE Yuletide spirit wasn't exactly flowing from Celtic Park as the festive season reached full swing.

McCann was dubbed 'Mr Scrooge' for his 'bah, humbug' approach to the annual celebrations for the players and staff.

His refusal to allow partners to join the official Christmas party led to a boycott by many players who decided they would have their own bash. And they did.

Meanwhile, McCann twiddled with his chicken drumsticks wondering if Santa would be good to him and provide him with the buyers he needed for the shares' issue to be a success.

New Year arrived and it seemed as if the offer was beginning to take off. It also seemed as if the players had forgiven their Mr Scrooge as the club's internationalists, John Collins, Paul McStay, Peter Grant and Pat Bonner backed the call with hard cash.

They led the way by digging deep into their own pockets to support the shares sell with Collins saying: 'It's a good thing to do and it's something I can hand on to my children. It's also nice to know that you've got a small part of the club which is, I'm sure, the way everyone will feel '

Parkhead spokesman Peter McLean kept the ball rolling with the comment: 'It's certainly heartening for us that some of our top stars have decided to invest in the club.' He then confirmed that the Celtic fans were coughing up in huge amounts to support their team in the historic offer before the 24 January deadline.

McLean said they had received more than 7,000 telephone inquiries on a special hotline number and added: 'We also had 25,000 on our mailing list for the prospectus – including all of our 18,000 season-ticket-holders – and the results have been incredible.'

Open days had also been popular and had brought in a lot of money. McLean, appearing more and more like Santa's little helper, beamed: 'On our first one we had more than 1,000 people there to see a video display telling them all about the club and our aims for the future. That day, coincidentally, was when we announced the signing of Pierre van Hooijdonk, which helped produce an incredible response of £178,000 for the share offer.

'Later, we had another evening at the park and in three hours, during which we again outlined the future, we took in £90,000.' Two more open evenings were lined up. He pointed out that the Ordinary share price of £62 was below the actual net asset value of £73.74 per share. Better was to come. The headlines stated that CELTIC'S SHARE ISSUE HAS THROWN PARKHEAD INTO CHAOS.

The club became inundated with so many requests for their new share prospectus that they had to bring in extra staff to cope.

Parkhead PR man Peter McLean popped back up with: 'Our open-day meetings have been tremendously well supported so far, but the interest has now gone through the roof. We have another three meetings for supporters at Parkhead and that will be the final opportunity for fans to invest before the deadline for share dealing is reached.'

He added: 'We have been overwhelmed with the demand and staggered by one group in particular – the Greenock Supporters' Club – who pooled their resources and have bought an incredible £25,000 worth of shares.'

The weekend of the three open days at Celtic Park drew in a staggering £1 million plus which prompted even more spoutings from the omnipresent PR man.

He announced: 'Everyone associated with the club is delighted at how incredibly successful the operation has been. To draw in that amount of money at the ground over Friday, Saturday and Sunday was incredible.'

The club had originally set a target of £5 million when the share issue was launched. That was quickly extended to £9 million. Tommy Burns had joined his star players by buying some shares in the hope, perhaps, that he could at last see some of the millions coming back to him to strengthen the team.

The last-minute rush from investors pushed the club over its target of £9 million. The response was so good that the fans were told they may be given another opportunity to buy a stake in Celtic's future at a later date.

Delighted club chiefs said they had chalked up a greater share issue than even they had hoped for.

Glasgow stockbrokers Greig Middleton said they would underwrite the share issue to the tune of £3 million while £4 million would come from Ireland via Dermot Desmond's QFS Financial Services and, in addition to the shares cash, a £1 million loan from major shareholder Eddie Keane was to be used to buy players – repayable on 15 December 1995.

But the words of McLean and others at Celtic during the first few weeks of the shares launch were not wholly accurate.

The first problem, not disclosed by Celtic, was that Dermot Desmond had only agreed to a £4 million offer if the other directors matched that amount between them.

It was down to Celtic director Willie Haughey to use his experience and influence at the time to save the club from a potential embarrassment.

McCann initially refused to put any more money in, saying he'd invested everything he was willing to. Only three other directors were in any position to raise the money, Michael McDonald, who represented Gerald Weisfeld, put up £1 million, Eddie Keane through Dominic put up another £1 million, John Keane and Willie Haughey put in £750,000 each. They convinced McCann to put up the other £500,000 simply to show solidarity. He did, reluctantly, and insisted that he get the first chance of a return on his investment.

But it didn't end there. McCann had encountered another problem. Haughey recalled: 'Fergus had allowed eight weeks for the shares sale but after six weeks he was struggling to sell them. Then I went to public meetings arranged with the fans to explain things and to try and find out why they weren't buying.

'I told them: "I don't believe you guys. Having waited 106 years you now have the opportunity to buy a stake in the club. What's going on?"

'It turned out it was the financial statements which had them confused. Fergus was always one for talking in financial terms, and the fans had got the wrong idea about what the underwriting of the shares by the big investors actually meant. They thought the shares had already been sold at that stage when the announcement was made. They didn't realise it merely meant the big investors were ready to step in if the fans didn't.

'I explained things to them and that's when we made what I regard as the quantum leap, with £2 million coming in over a weekend of meetings with the fans and our own group agreeing to match the Dermot Desmond offer.'

Within the space of those eight weeks, some 10,000 supporters bought shares and became part-owners of Celtic.

McCann was like the cat that had got the cream and he was licking and savouring every last drop of it. There was the extra bonus for McCann with the news that the shares issue had been oversubscribed to the tune of an astonishing £4.5 million in addition to the £8.5 million originally forecast. In other words, almost a third more shares than were on offer were sought by the fans and other investors.

It was the most successful shares offer ever in British football. But although McCann was at last a happy man, the fans weren't exactly celebrating. They had used their hard-earned cash to boost funds at the club and they wanted to see success in return.

Having a new stadium rising like a phoenix from the old

Celtic Park was a sight to behold, but not as comforting or as emotional a sight as the raising of a silver trophy in the hands of the players. Success on the park was what the supporters wanted and now, as shareholders, demanded.

Managing Director McCann was not as forthcoming about how the cash would be spent. This caused many a nervous twitch among the Parkhead faithful.

After the news of the shares success, McCann said: 'The fans will assume that we will handle the money properly and it could very well be the case that the funding will be used to meet the requirements of the needs that Tommy Burns identifies. But they will also know that we have to have better facilities. It is a concern that, as the stadium rebuilding continues, we will have only 34,000 seats next season.'

In an apparent afterthought to try and appease the fans, he added: 'There have been a lot of things missing in the last few years but we now see no reason why we cannot compete, not only with Rangers, but with any big club in Britain.'

Tommy Burns had been promised around £4 million and, by the time of the shares' issue, he had been allowed to spend little more than the £1.2 million for the purchase of the big Dutch striker Pierre van Hooijdonk.

It was to be a constant source of frustration and conflict between the manager and his boss, but, with his obvious joy over the shares success, there was only one partnership which really mattered Fergus McCann at that point.

His love match with lawyer Elspeth Campbell was about to become a little more permanent. Friday, 27 January 1995, was the day when McCann put all thoughts of football business out of his mind to concentrate on wedding business as he was married at St Margaret's Church in Ayr.

Celtic players and directors were conspicuous by their absence. Only a small number of family and friends braved the winter conditions with Miss Campbell's mother Effie, a retired Church of Scotland minister, joking with media photographers as she posed in her striking blue outfit.

McCann – minus his bunnet – appeared a little nervous as he arrived for the short ceremony.

The service was a joint affair with a Catholic priest and a Protestant minister sharing the duties.

It was the minister who introduced a little light relief into the affair by saying: 'For you both, this is the first day of the rest of your lives. For you, Fergus, if you'll pardon the pun, this is a whole new ball game.'

But the real ball game was only just hotting up.

SIX

Good and Bad

THERE was, and probably ever will be, only one thing on the minds of the Celtic supporters, be they shareholders or not. Victory. Pure, simple, satisfying. But, despite the finances looking in better shape at Celtic Park, the team didn't. They had just lost the first Old Firm encounter of 1995 at the Ne'er Day match and Burns was just as frustrated as the fans.

McCann didn't appear to bother. He was still in his counting house with all the money and planning where it should be spent; bricks and mortar seemed a better bet to him than expensive foreign signings.

He frequently cast an envious eye westwards over the city to Ibrox Park, home of Celtic's fiercest and oldest rivals, where he had recently watched Rangers win the game against Celtic.

He had seen the new-look Ibrox with its 50,000 all-seated stadium. While he was there, the Celtic chief not only checked out the opposition's stadium, he also checked out the opposition.

His counterpart, Rangers' owner and chairman David Murray, recalls the moment quite vividly.

He said: 'The first time I met him was when he came to an Old Firm match at Ibrox. It was the first meeting between us. I had seen him previously – the first time on television on the steps of Parkhead at the takeover. I had also heard him on radio talking about the old dynasty and how they wouldn't talk to him. It was difficult to make any real first impression of the guy then.

'At Ibrox he came into the boardroom with his trademark moustache and bunnet. It was pretty obvious from his manner that he was trying to work out who were the good guys and who were the bad guys.

'There really wasn't an awful lot said between us, and I really don't think that, at that stage, he had realised what he had taken on. I was concerned at that because I knew how it affected me when I took over at Rangers. It takes over your whole life. But he hadn't a clue at that stage.

'I lived in Edinburgh and that was a benefit to me. For McCann to choose to live in Glasgow and think he could live an ordinary, everyday life, he must have been kidding himself. He was too accessible to the fans and to the media.

'I am seen as David Murray, Edinburgh businessman. Fergus was seen as Celtic Football Club chairman and nothing else. He came in as a complete stranger and he didn't know who to trust.

'The first thing about him was he said he would be there for five years and do this, that and the other. In the main, he did, I suppose, do just that despite the criticism.

'He'd been in the job about a year and I had spoken to him and suggested we should try and work a little closer together.

'As chairmen of football clubs we both had the hopes, beliefs and aspirations of so many people to contend with.

'The first night we actually sat down together was when I invited him to dinner. It was at Cosmos in Edinburgh [which Murray owns].

'He came through on the train from Glasgow. We talked about our beliefs and hopes and the way forward. We had very similar agendas – except he was going after a five-year period and I was staying.

'I don't think the way he went about things in a purely professional business sense was wrong, but it was on the public relations side where he fell.

'We didn't have any great, meaningful discussion, it was more about us getting to know each other a little better. There weren't that many other meetings between us after that.'

McCann's dream of achieving similar, if not greater, success as a club to that enjoyed by Rangers over recent years, was slowly becoming a reality.

But much more had still to be done and that was something the new financial man whom McCann had appointed to Celtic Park knew only too well.

Marketing director Patrick Ferrell had come from a successful business background. Ferrell, 47, was a former director of the international group Gold Corporation and he was expected to bring the Midas touch with him.

He was already enjoying some success at Parkhead having increased the season-ticket sales from around 7,000 to 18,500 within the first McCann season.

His remit was tickets, sponsorships, corporate sales, media sales, all retail sales, Celtic pools and catering.

As he surveyed the rebuilding work at Celtic Park, Ferrell realised then that the team would soon be playing back home and not at Hampden.

He said at the time: 'We will finish this work on schedule and it will be the best stadium in the land.' But he also admitted, in March 1995, that it would probably take Celtic another five years to get back to the top alongside Rangers.

He added: 'That is being realistic. We have had to not only build the foundations of a new stadium but also a new business. Celtic was badly managed for decades, not just years but decades, and the business was very run down.

'This was the one-time most-successful team in the UK, a world-class football club, which was not exploited the way it should have been. We are still looking at the Lisbon Lions as our claim to fame, and, although we are very proud of them, that was way back in 1967 when they won the European Cup.

'Celtic are experiencing the problems Rangers did, but Rangers came back and we are going along that same road. We are running against the clock and, yes, everyone compares us to Rangers, but the only way for us now is up.

'The response to the share offer was overwhelming and reaffirmed that Celtic have the most loyal support in the world. Who else would plough cash into a club that had suffered such a drought as ours? They recognised the opportunity and wanted to be in at the start of the new adventure.

'But, at the end of the day, the fans want trophies and that's understandable. The team is the locomotive that pulls the train.'

Fergus McCann may have been regarded as the 'Fat Controller' in charge of that train and the carriages it pulled, but he was quite happy to take a back seat as he recalled his first year in office.

The Herald's Ian Paul dubbed him 'courageous' for having stumped up hard-earned cash for Celtic, taken over the driving seat and given up 50 years of bachelorhood into the bargain.

McCann gave himself eight out of ten in the first term report card.

One had to assume that the Tommy Burns issue, past and present at that time, was one of the minus points.

McCann said: 'We have a good system here. It is up to the manager to get any employment or transfer deals approved. He has a budget like everyone else in the organisation. He knows what the guidelines are and he has a lot of power and authority within that.'

At least he admitted: 'If you look at what a manager at a

club like this has to cover, it is staggering. He has to have a coaching staff, a youth-development staff, he has a first team, reserve teams, youth teams and a boys' club network. He has to attend to training plans and he has also to be a man-manager dealing with all these individuals. Plus he has to be available to the press, the sponsors and the supporters.

'He has all of these demands upon his time and, when it comes to deals for games or transfers or contracts, most managers nowadays would prefer to be one step away. Their main concern is getting the best out of players and they already have a pretty big job as it is.

'If Burns wishes to buy a player, he tells us what he thinks he wants to spend out of his budget. Then it is up to myself or any director to put the pieces together with the other party and deliver what he wants. But it is not always possible.'

Tommy Burns didn't need to be told that and certainly not by Fergus McCann.

But Burns remained diplomatic saying: 'The football decisions are left to me within the resources Fergus can provide. We respect each other's views and we're both working for the good of Celtic.'

As far as Celtic's dispute with Kilmarnock over Burns was concerned, McCann still arrogantly believed he was in the right.

He said: 'We did nothing wrong. That is the whole point. My only regret is that Celtic have been badly treated. The appeal at the League just now is not really an appeal because the committee, elected by the clubs, is asking their representatives if they are backing them or McCann. That is not an appeal hearing.

'My special concern is that a football organisation, the SFA, has taken upon itself a constitution that puts it above the law. For any organisation to claim that power is a very dangerous thing in any society. Only within the last 18 months has the clause been brought into the constitution which forbids any person to go to court against them. He has to give up that legal right and this is with the blessing of FIFA.

'I believe there is something rotten when that happens. It leaves it open to abuse. I think the fine of £100,000 imposed on us is an abuse of that power. In fact, we could all have been sentenced to hang because there is no limit to what can be imposed.

'But let me emphasise that Celtic have always fitted in with the football structure and we will always be big supporters of the SFA as we have been in the past.'

For McCann, there were two other unexpected issues during his first year in power: 'I knew there would be media attention but I did not believe it could be quite as excessive as it was. I have also found the sheer intensity of people trying to help, even within the club, to be surprising. It's good that they care, but there are drawbacks when they are quite so committed.'

Not long after his comments, the club was ordered to pay Kilmarnock £200,000 in compensation by the tribunal set up to resolve the issue.

That ruling meant McCann, as he himself predicted to Frank Cairney when 'poaching' Burns, did indeed end up with a bill of £300,000 – more than the amount he had feared he would have to pay out to Kilmarnock if he had settled earlier. The fact remained that it cost him an extra £150,000 plus legal costs by dragging the matter on so long in what was always going to be a losing battle.

Kilmarnock chairman Bob Fleeting was jubilant. He said: 'I am delighted this matter is finally over. I cannot comment on the mechanics of the tribunal, which was private, but we are obviously pleased at the way the affair has been handled and pleased with the compensation figure.

'This club has always recognised that Celtic are one of

the world's greatest clubs and it is a pity things had to go so far. The relationship between the two clubs has been damaged but not irreparably. It is now my job to ensure that the damage can be repaired. But I have to admit it is a sorry day when you have to go to these lengths.

'Now it has to be hoped that everyone at Rugby Park will recognise the contribution made to this club by Tommy Burns and Billy Stark. We should all welcome them when they return here next season with their new club.'

From Celtic Park McCann issued a much briefer statement. He said: 'We are disappointed with the costly result to Celtic of the tribunal and the Scottish Football League's decision in this matter. However, we are pleased that the issue has been concluded.'

But there were still more troubles for Celtic and McCann building up on the horizon.

AS Celtic entered the close season towards the end of May 1995, the silent battle between McCann and Burns was beginning to gain voice.

Celtic were back in a cup final – again, against what would normally be considered inferior opposition. They were playing in the Tennents Scottish Cup-final clash with Airdrie at Hampden.

During one of the pre-match press conferences, Parkhead boss Burns had been quizzed about prospective signings and snapped back: 'You'll have to ask Mr McCann about that!'

He refused to enlarge on the statement, but there was no doubt he was becoming increasingly frustrated at the failure to conclude financial deals with stars he had identified as his priority targets – these included Belgium international Marc Degryse of Anderlecht, who was believed to have been offered *less* money by Celtic than he was earning in Belgium.

The comments prompted a swift move by Celtic to defuse reports of an 'explosive' row between manager Tommy Burns and chief executive Fergus McCann.

Burns had clearly said all he was going to say on the matter, but McCann issued a statement outlining his ambitions. And he strenuously defended efforts to sign new players.

McCann spoke at the end of the long-running compensation row with Kilmarnock saying: 'The type of players we are aiming to sign involves working in a new market place which is extremely competitive. Celtic's aim is to bring top-class international players to the club and to do that we must compete with the top clubs in the world.

'Tommy Burns has identified a number of suitable players to me. We are working hard to conclude signings. I have made five journeys to Europe in the last few weeks. Negotiations are proceeding well.

'However, these are not assisted by agents and others using the press to widen the markets for their players by issuing negative and misleading stories, heightening the awareness of their ability and lobbying to raise the price.

'The international market place for top-class players includes many issues such as contracts, currencies, visas, agents, lawyers, advisers, tax status, previous obligations and, in some cases, even a third or fourth club. Hence the length of time negotiations can take.

'In the past, the club has rushed into decisions and bought players for amounts widely regarded as in excess of their value. I don't want to get involved in discussing individual names – the time for that is when you have signed a player – rather than heightening the expectations of supporters, only to possibly disappoint them through no lack of finance or ambition.

'Celtic Football Club will sign top-class players and will not be pressurised into panic-buying. The one thing the whole club and support should focus on now is to give Tommy Burns and players complete support as we work together to win Celtic's first trophy for six years.' A few days later and the drought was over.

Celtic had beaten Airdrie by the narrowest of margins, 1–0. But the simmering feud between manager Burns and McCann was obvious. Burns had had enough of what he regarded as McCann's determination to be heavily involved in purely football matters, while McCann saw it as simply protecting his interests and the interests of the club.

But he was underestimating the determination and the toughness of Tommy Burns. Burns was willing to compromise, listen and take advice, but he was not willing to be pushed into a corner – especially after having shown outstanding management qualities.

He had lifted his players from the pits of despair after their Coca-Cola Cup-final defeat by Raith Rovers. Now, he saw them re-emerge as winners and he wanted the chance to go further without the hassle from McCann.

As Burns said after the game: 'The pressure was unbearable. We didn't play particularly well at all, but our support stood by us and I have to thank them for that. The result was always going to be paramount and the players will get a huge lift from it. Now they know how it feels to win and they'll want to enjoy it in the future.'

But, only two days later, the speculation within the media was that Burns was set to quit because of the rift with McCann.

They posed outside Hampden on Saturday with the Tennents Scottish Cup but it emerged that they had been communicating by memo recently.

There had been several times during the season when Burns was on the verge of walking out after differences of opinion with McCann.

Burns said: 'The only way this can be resolved is by talking and listening to each other's viewpoint.

'It will not be like the gunfight at the OK Corral but we have to get the ground rules laid once and for all. I think I have been quoted as saying I would resign which is probably not right. To resign because of difficulties I have encountered here would let down a lot of people who support the club.

'To resign would be the easy way out. I'll make it my business to let the fans know what's going on.'

Burns was also angry that his players were left lounging about in a hotel during a pre-Cup visit to Milan because McCann had vetoed spending money on activities to occupy the players' leisure time.

Burns said: 'They have been treated like second-class citizens instead of the most important people at Celtic, which they were when I was a player. It has embarrassed and annoyed me. There is a fantastic challenge here and we have a long way to go. To do that, the people who run the club must trust me to manage the way I think the job should be done. I've carried this on my back for some time.'

But McCann took a different tack, if a predictable one, saying: 'The state of affairs between Burns and myself is fine. Tommy has a strong personality and his own ideas and so have I. Obviously, we have had disagreements, but we have the same objectives, and he knows he has my backing.'

What Burns really wanted was cash to boost the playing side. He wanted the freedom to run the football side of the business without having to refer to McCann at every stage. That was the agreement when Burns returned to Parkhead to replace Lou Macari. But it had clearly not been fulfilled.

Despite all the comments and rumours, McCann remained determined and detached. He said: 'Everything concerning raising capital and organising players' contracts is my area and I leave him to handle the football. It is a learning process for Tommy and myself. We have only been in the job a year and Celtic are a big club.'

Despite his comments, the feud grew and became even more public when the man Burns replaced – Lou Macari – gave him his backing.

Macari knew better than anyone the torment Burns was going through and suggested it was identical to his own troubled relationship with McCann.

He also warned Burns that he had got the boot for telling the club chief to mind his own business in team matters.

Macari, then manager at Stoke City, said: 'McCann sacked me because I stood up to him, so I'm not surprised Tommy's found working with the guy too much. The similarities with my problems with Fergus are obvious. I went through the same routine. I wanted more money to spend on the team and never got it. I challenged him and ended up out of a job. I responded by letter to one of his famous memos, telling him to let me get on with the job of running the team and that I was in charge. He didn't like it and he sacked me.

'Forget all the stuff that's been put out about me not being at Parkhead enough. That was never an issue. The real reason was that I told him not to interfere.'

Macari said the battle for money at Parkhead was still the same 12 months down the line. He added: 'I told McCann the team needed major surgery and that new players were required. I have been proved right.

'McCann never gave me a penny to spend. In my time at Celtic I spent £800,000 on transfers – but I had to sell Gerry Creaney to Portsmouth to get that cash. I tried to sign Alan McLoughlin from Portsmouth. I had four hours to sign a player. But the deal didn't go through because McCann wouldn't allow me to back my judgement. Yet he knows nothing about football.'

Burns had expected the 'lion's share' – to quote McCann

– of the successful £14 million share issue to improve the team. But it wasn't happening.

The public row had reached the stage where rumours were sweeping the streets that Burns had decided to quit even though the manager had indicated that he would rather stay in the job and fight for what he believed in.

The media appeared to be on his side. *The Herald's* Ken Gallacher summed up the Burns row stating:

> Burns has the support and trust of major investors at the club but there is some unhappiness that behind-the-scenes disputes have been aired in public. Powerful voices at Parkhead do not want to see a re-run of internecine warfare, which came close to destroying the club under the former regime.
>
> If McCann were to consider sacking Burns, who has just brought the first trophy to the club in six years, he could find opposition from supporters and, possibly, major investors. As for the fans, they are behind Burns, and if anything were to damage the manager then season-ticket sales would slump and McCann's financial strategy could be in jeopardy.
>
> Basically, McCann must learn to live with Burns and how football goes about its business in Scotland. If he does not do so then the Celtic saviour may find himself facing a kind of conflict which the club cannot afford.
>
> All Burns wants to do is manage the club the way it was done when he was a player and when the club knew almost constant success. The people who invested their money in the Celtic share issue, people whose feelings cannot be ignored, would not see much wrong with that.

There were, however, some directors who felt Burns was wrong to take the gloss off their Cup-final success by

Still wearing the
bonnet – at least
it's a Celtic one

Out on a limb as
McCann meets
the press

One of McCann's first sacking announcements: the departure
of Lou Macari. Dominic Keane and Jack McGinn (one of
the old board) were soon to depart the club themselves

More of the good old days: the directors' line-up of (*left to right*) Dominic
Keane, Tom Grant, Fergus McCann and Brian Dempsey

Only hours after McCann walked through the doors at Celtic Park and almost blew the final deal. Here, apparently happy, he poses with members of his new board. *Left to right*: Tom Grant, Brian Dempsey, Fergus McCann, Jack McGinn, Dominic Keane, John Keane and Jimmy Farrell. Only John Keane actually survived McCann's reign

The crowds gather outside and wait for the new board to emerge

ABOVE: Former manager Tommy Burns shares one of the few lighter moments with McCann at a press conference. Their relationship was to end in controversial circumstances

RIGHT: New Celtic manager Dr Jozef Venglos is presented to the media. He left at the end of the 1998–99 season. *Left to right*: Jock Brown, Jozef Venglos, Fergus McCann and Eric Black

The unfurling of the League flag in August 1998 when Fergus McCann
was booed by the faithful

Celtic fans rejoice at the 5–1 victory over Rangers in November 1998

Player of the Year Henrik Larsson deceives the Aberdeen defence

Vidar Riseth congratulates Mark Viduka on another goal

LEFT: McCann's Montreal residence

BELOW: Kanawaki Golf Club in Montreal. McCann was a member there in 1994

McCann's winter residence in Scottsdale, Arizona

The view from McCann's villa in Bermuda

speaking out against McCann's 'interference' in team affairs. But they refused to sanction moves against the manager.

The directors held a board meeting at which the issue was top of the agenda. Most of them were astounded that Burns chose to speak out the way he did and when he did. But there was no support for McCann's counter-attack, either.

And there, on the wing, was one Brian Dempsey. Whether he liked it or not, he was again being punted as the fans' favourite to move in on the board and bring some stability to the runaway McCann train.

But Dempsey, although still keen to become involved at some stage, was not in any rush to return to the public arena which Celtic had found itself wallowing in again.

Dempsey, who was abroad on business at the time, was backed by the fans and by Professor Hugh Drake, chairman of the old Celtic Shareholders Association.

Drake said: 'McCann has sidelined us by forming his own shareholders society, but we still represent most of the shareholders involved in Celtic before the coup.

'I think Brian Dempsey has all the skills needed by the club, and I would like to see him back at Celtic. We backed Fergus and Brian at the time as they were the dream ticket. The coup may have saved Celtic's body but it hasn't saved its soul.

'We had high hopes of Fergus McCann, but he hasn't taken the advice offered to him. There is a lack of wise counsel at Celtic. The club has become a corporate entity rather than a football entity. It is briefcases rather than boots.'

But Dempsey would not be tempted at that stage. He said: 'Shareholders and other fans have been calling me and asking for my support. They have always had my support and they will continue to do so.

'But I am unwilling to get involved at this particular time

although, as a supporter myself, I am staying well briefed.'

McCann didn't want Dempsey back either. He had successfully frozen Dempsey out and he didn't want that particular thorn back in his flesh – no matter how the fans felt.

So it was McCann who attempted to defuse the situation. He offered a new deal to Burns in a bid to cement up the cracks that threatened the manager's brief career with the club.

But it emerged that Burns, already frustrated by the pace of transfer negotiations, could end up selling before he started buying.

International midfielder John Collins announced he may have played his last game for Celtic. Targeted signing Marc Degryse of Anderlecht, said he wouldn't go to Glasgow, while Celtic and Spurs dismissed speculation over a £2 million bid for striker Pierre van Hooijdonk whose Scottish Cup winner against Airdrie ended Celtic's six-year trophy famine.

Burns apologised for his post-Cup final outburst and said he was not keen to start breaking up a cup-winning side so early. He said: 'When I came here I said our top priority was not simply to win something but to do so on a regular basis. We want to return to the highest level and bring back the days when Celtic supporters had finals and vital league games to look forward to every season.

'We are all working towards making Celtic a great club and Parkhead a place to be feared again by the opposition. That win has only brought an end to a six-year barren spell. We must now show the fans that we can be winners every season. The players are determined to make Celtic Park a place where our supporters can come to enjoy attractive, attacking play.'

THE faithful Celtic fans were more prone to lift their eyes to the skies through sheer frustration than prayer. They thought the days of seeking divine intervention in their club were long gone. They were, after all, the bad old days. These were the good new days. Well, that's what they thought as the former board packed their cardboard boxes and left – complete with the infamous 'biscuit tin'.

Now, it seemed, the biscuit tin had taken on a new guise in the form of one Fergus McCann, and it wasn't long before the supporters' voices were once again raised in anger.

With Burns expressing his views, albeit with more of a whimper than a bellow, the real voice at Celtic Park – the fans – began to grow in volume.

The first major warning came from a raging Celtic Supporters' chief Gerry Madden. He responded to questions from the press with a shot across the bows of the good ship Celtic with words that even McCann didn't really expect to hear – at least not that soon after the takeover.

Madden, speaking on behalf of the massive Parkhead support, told McCann: 'It won't take the fans long to turn against you.'

The Parkhead punters were still coming to terms with another summer transfer shocker after bitter rivals Rangers pinched Gordan Petric from under their noses. And Madden – whose phone was white-hot with furious Celtic supporters demanding explanations – rapped: 'The fans have already watched the people upstairs destroy the club in the past. They won't accept false promises again.

'Everybody seems to be talking about the money at Parkhead being Fergus McCann's, but it's the supporters' money. We have now ploughed £20 million into the club in season-tickets over the last two years and the share issue, so it's about time some of our money was spent.

'We were told Tommy Burns would be getting the lion's

share of that money, but it's obvious there is still a rift between him and the chief executive when it comes to signing players.' Madden reckoned that after the Petric fiasco the club would be held to an even bigger ransom when they eventually signed some big-name players.

The fans' leader said: 'We are now going to be ripped off for players everywhere we go. It's obvious to everyone that Celtic are desperate to get some new faces. Now with the snubs we've had, it's going to get worse.

'Clubs and players know Celtic will pay just about anything now to get players, and it's all been caused by the fact that we wouldn't lay out cash earlier in the season when we tried to sign Marc Degryse. He wasn't going to cost all that much, but ended up signing for Sheffield Wednesday.'

Most fans believed that Celtic needed to sign a player of the stature of former Rangers captain Terry Butcher, who started the influx of big stars into Ibrox almost a decade before.

Madden added: 'When Rangers signed Butcher, they had to pay high finance for him, but it became a snowball effect and top players started coming to the club. We have to try and emulate that. Fergus is playing with fire because the supporters want to know exactly what is going on and I don't think it would be too long before they turn on him – just like they did with the old regime.

'Every time we turn a corner it just gets worse, and I can understand that some Celtic fans might snap. Even when we won the Cup final in May the gloss was taken off by Tommy Burns and Fergus McCann falling out the next Monday. Since then it's just been bad publicity after bad publicity. Obviously we don't want to see people staying away from the club, but I think Fergus McCann should really start thinking about delivering something to the fans.'

McCann's reaction was not to go and spend money, it

was to give the now-rare interviews to the press where he could put his side of the story – as, and when he chose. This time he chose to say he liked Tommy Burns. He even told *Evening Times* journalist Alan Davidson that he reckoned Burns to be a good manager.

But as Celtic approached a new season, and arguably the most challenging period in the club's history, there remained a heavy whiff of a conflict of interests between McCann, the managing director and major shareholder, and Burns, the manager, former player and eternal supporter. Davidson wrote: 'Whether or not the two men – who fell out publicly at the end of last season – can ever resolve what appear to be inherent differences remains to be seen. Whether or not they can continue to work together is a subject up for grabs. Tomorrow, next week, next month, next year it might all fall apart. What is likely is the abrasive effect of two driven personalities. There is more than the possibility of full-scale combustion.'

McCann's thoughts on the relationship between football's chief executives and their managers made for interesting reading at the time. He said: 'A lot of what are termed football people are not particularly aware. It can be difficult for them to recognise there must be a structure if there is to be a successful organisation whose target is to run a club capable of playing the game of football successfully.

'With Tommy Burns I think we have a good professional relationship. I don't always agree with him and, in turn, he doesn't always agree with me. The way I look at it, we are growing together in this business and at this club.

'What we do have in common is the prosperity of Celtic. We don't have the same kind of personality, and there are times when I think he can get a bit emotional. We have to remember he is in a highly pressurised job. A lot of demands are placed upon him from all sorts of angles and all sorts of people, and I am aware of that.

'But do I have regrets in appointing him as the club's manager? No, I don't. He has led the team to a Scottish Cup success, our first trophy in six years, and he is committed to success. Just as I am.'

Asked to explain why Celtic managed just one major close-season signing, Andreas Thom, despite the fact he was on record as saying his manager would enjoy the lion's share of the £14 million earned from the share issue, McCann said: 'To be accurate, around £10 million was raised by our fans via the share issue. I don't think I used the expression the 'lion's share' – although I did say the manager would be given a fair proportion of it for new players.

'We can't use Rangers as a basis for our operation. We can't be driven by what they do. We have to recognise Rangers have had a head start on us for a number of years. My responsibility is to put together a future for Celtic and not to work on some kind of knee-jerk reaction because of what Rangers have done or may do in the future.

'Sure, I want further investment in players, and there will be others coming to the club. I'm not about to quote figures but Thom will certainly be one of Britain's highest-paid players, and that says something about our ambition. But, you know, the best manager in the land, no matter the field he works in, is not necessarily the manager who spends the most. He is the manager who does the best with the available resources.

'Over the past year we have generated some £25 million and £17 million has been spent on the construction of our new stand. We have spent around £6 million on players also. A balance has to be struck. We can't have everything at once. I believe in this club and its future, otherwise I wouldn't have come here from Canada and put a lot of money into it.'

The future, as far as McCann was concerned, was only five years long in footballing terms.

He said: 'I don't think anyone should go into a job of this intensity for more than five years. It just wouldn't be smart. At my age I don't want to make a long-term career.

'I have other things to do with my life and, when my time is up here, I will go back to my home in Bermuda, play some golf and live a healthier life.

'I've no regrets about the job, but what I do regret, is people writing stories for stories' sake. There was the suggestion that someone was killed on the construction site, the television gantry was declared unsafe, Celtic forgot about television arrangements and there were demonstrations from the locals. If you believed all those things then you wouldn't be believing anything that was true.

'It's the same with all the transfer stories, all blown out of proportion. Tommy Burns has maybe made enquiries about 50 players in 50 weeks but that doesn't mean he has made bids for them.

'I think, given a reasonable degree of success, we should be able to make a profit next year and that will be reinvested in players. We want to generate the cash from a full stadium to buy new players. In fact, if we didn't have the problem of virtually starting from scratch and building a new stadium then we would be right up there with Rangers in terms of buying.'

But right then the only thing McCann was buying was time. Time to build a new stadium and a money-making company. A company that would make him money and lots of it.

Oh, and there was one other thing . . . making money out of the fans. And there was another way he saw of doing just that. A way that was to prove naïve, downright foolish and dangerous to the point where it threatened the very core of Celtic's financial and business credibility.

It was, according to two former directors, a move which almost brought about the downfall of Celtic.

SEVEN

For Sale

DURING yet another winter of discontent with the Celtic players, and many fans, now regarding Christmas as Scroogemas, McCann had money on his mind once again.

This time it was raised through a rather tenuous connection with an old Tory, former Aberdeen MP Albert McQuarrie. Through his recommendation a bright, young, silver-tongued financial salesman found himself with a tremendous money-making opportunity. Sell insurance and related business through Celtic. Great potential. Great profit. Great work if you can get it.

And he did . . . because there was one great ingredient the great McCann had a great taste for – great money.

The MP, Albert McQuarrie, born on New Year's Day in 1918, was older than any of the Celtic directors, let alone the old board. He spoke to Eric Reilly, the new Celtic financial director, and recommended a young man by the name of Paul Goodwin – a whiz-kid in financial circles. The fact he was also the nephew of the late and great Celtic legend Jock Stein probably had a lot do to with both Reilly being taken in and McCann being convinced.

Goodwin was only 28 years old. But he managed to convince the 'experienced' at Celtic Park that he was the man for them. The man who could and would earn money for the club.

The Glasgow-based money man had apparently turned his back on playing football to play football financially.

In 1990 at the age of 22 he set up a firm called Caledonian Investments and quickly established a client base of 300 firms and a turnover of around £500,000 a year.

Three years later he was hitting the big time and, in his eyes, there was nothing bigger than Celtic.

Through McQuarrie and Goodwin's own Celtic past he was able to work his way into the club.

Goodwin then set up a second firm called Caledonian Services Ltd, which he used to front the franchise from Celtic selling insurance, mortgages and PEPs (Personal Equity Plans) on behalf of the company.

Reilly and McCann were won over with the prospect of a £300,000 sponsorship package from Caledonian and a further £100,000 in the first year through insurance commission.

On car insurance alone, Goodwin's firm received more than 10,000 inquiries since the link with Celtic began in January 1996. And, with average home gates of 35,000 and many more thousands on Celtic's mailing list, the potential was enormous. Then he brought ahead plans for home and property insurance.

McCann said at the time that, with Celtic aiming to compete at the highest level, income had to be generated from commercial activities. He added that the Celtic PEP was a tax-free investment opportunity would not only benefit supporters but would also help the club generate funds.

But the credentials of the first man in Celtic's history to be allowed to use the club's great name for a private commercial enterprise were obviously not checked – despite concerns expressed by Celtic director and financial expert Dominic Keane.

Goodwin, who lived in a luxurious villa in East Kilbride and had a mansion in Bothwell complete with a £20,000 stocked wine cellar, was already on the slippery slope.

Within four months the financial world was buzzing with rumours concerning Goodwin and his activities. It seemed he was suffering financially himself and was playing fast and loose with clients' money.

Financial regulators Fimbra and the fraud squad were already looking into the affairs of his investment business. Fimbra ordered Caledonian to suspend its investment activities pending an investigation.

The order, said Fimbra, was to protect investors because the firm had been unable to demonstrate that it had dealt with a client's money within the rules. Goodwin claimed it had been an oversight, but Fimbra used a fast-track procedure reserved for serious cases.

Goodwin played it down as a 'lapse' by his firm and described it as 'an isolated incident' which had taken place two years previously.

His firm, he said, was co-operating with Fimbra and holding its own internal inquiry. The client had made four investments through Caledonian totalling £80,000. The first three had been duly made but the fourth – and largest – had not. Goodwin said the client would be satisfied that the 'lost' funds were replaced and any missing interest made good.

The alarm bells did not seem to ring at Celtic even then. It was weeks later – as the Goodwin bandwagon began to crash – that Reilly and McCann sensed the impending doom at last.

It wasn't until the second week of June 1996 that Celtic decided to terminate its contract with Caledonian. In a statement, the club said the investment policies Celtic fans had through Celtic Investment Services and Celtic Insurance Services – the trading names for Caledonian – were secure and there was no need for concern. Most of the policies had been placed with major insurance firms who would honour them.

Four days later Caledonian Investments went into liquidation. The liquidator described the company as 'insolvent' with little in the way of assets to cover liabilities. He made all 12 Caledonian employees redundant.

Three months later Goodwin was charged with fraud. It was another year before he appeared in court and was jailed for 18 months for attempting to defraud a retired couple out of £139,000 of insurance and two other fraud charges. His Celtic connections had not been able to save him.

According to both Willie Haughey and Dominic Keane – both Celtic directors at the time – it was an incredible and saga which did McCann no favours and showed the Celtic boss in a less than complimentary light: naïve, unconcerned and unmoved.

Neither Haughey nor Keane knew anything about the franchise until the deal was done.

Willie Haughey had been driving to Celtic Park when he heard an advertisement on the local radio station, Radio Clyde, relating to Celtic Insurance.

Haughey said: 'To say I was astounded was an understatement. I was absolutely flabbergasted

'Never in its 106-year history had Celtic ever sold its name to anyone, now here it was with a firm that few had ever heard of, and with no discussion having taken place involving directors of the football club such as me and Dominic.

'When I raised it at a board meeting I was told everything was okay and not to worry about it. It is not possible to say anything about the details of what was discussed then or how heated the meeting may have been, but, suffice it to say, the rest is history.'

Dominic Keane was equally astounded at the way McCann had allowed the franchise to go ahead at the time.

He said: 'I remember at the time we arrived one Saturday afternoon for a home game and I was coming out to my seat, I sat just beside Fergus and I looked around the stadium and all I could see was Celtic Insurance Services.

'There was even this special telephone number ending with 1967, our European Cup-winning year, and I thought to myself this must be some novelty thing to do with the match-day sponsors. Then the stadium announcer informed the fans about Celtic Insurance Services. There was a jingle and there were boards all around the stadium. I had never seen anything like it. I didn't know anything about it and I remember saying to Willie – he'd just come in at the time – "Who is this Celtic Insurance Services?" He looked around and said, "Never heard of them".

'We sat in our seats and I turned to Fergus, who had come in at this time and said, "What's going on here?" He gave me some sort of explanation like, "Yeah, yeah we were introduced to this guy, we'll get you this guy's name, he used to be an MP, I'll get you his name, up in Aberdeen. I can't remember his name. So we were introduced to this other guy and he'd set up insurances at £300,000 a year to Celtic, plus commissions." I said to Fergus, "They are using our name – who are they?"

'On the Monday I phoned Willie and said to him I wasn't happy with this firm using Celtic's name. We didn't know who they were and, over the weekend, I spoke to some people and to my accountants on the Monday and asked them to do a credit check on the company that was fronting Celtic Insurance Services.

'The report I got back was bad. I looked at it and I wasn't the least bit happy about it and I phoned Willie and I told him the same. It just didn't add up, with poor credit references and suggestions that it was a bad risk.

'We took the report in to Eric Reilly and told him we checked these people out and it didn't look good. He just said they seemed fine, that we had been introduced by this MP guy from Aberdeen, but he'd look into it.

'He said it was a good deal for us, it was going to be backed up by larger companies and this chap had great pedigree for direct selling etc. But I was concerned that they were using the Celtic name when even the old board never gave the name out – I mean you've got to be very careful if somebody is out masquerading under our name.

'I told him I didn't mind if it was Norwich Union or Prudential, but here was a company, this Caledonian Investment, which we knew nothing about.

'Eric wouldn't acknowledge that to us, so at the next board meeting, I think it was the following week, it was raised and we were told in the nicest possible way not to get involved as there wasn't really a problem.

'There was a discussion but we got short-changed. We were told it was an operational matter, it was a sponsorship arrangement and we weren't directly involved, it was only our name. You know what happened after that.

'I still believe, and I think Willie does too, and others within Celtic Park, that when it broke in the summer regarding that chap Goodwin – and I still believe that to this day – that it could have brought Celtic down, the good name of Celtic. The ramifications of that could have been disastrous. It didn't because one of the big insurance institutions pulled us out of it. God knows how much it's cost them to pick up the tab. Now that was only one example of a number of things which were going on without proper internal reviews of what they were. I think it was a quick sponsorship deal and I think we were very fortunate to get out of it.'

THE man who would be king at Celtic Park was now firmly settled in his Parkhead palace. But life outside the battlements of his East End fortress was not easy for McCann.

From within, and surrounded by his army of advisers and messengers, McCann could happily take on all comers within the football arena. But once he left and assumed the role of Mr McCann, father and home provider, things were a little more vulnerable for him. He was now three years into the job and his pending hat-trick in survival was acknowledged by various sections of the media.

The fact that he could now pick his time to speak and be interviewed by whom he chose to, and when it suited him, allowed McCann to drop his guard and give the fans a little more personal insight into the man who rode to victory over the old Celtic board on the crest of a rebel wave.

Here was a man who would have all believe that he was not an aggressor, agitator, dictator but a sensitive, caring, frightened individual.

A man described in interviews at the time as 'unmoved by flattery' and 'uncomfortable with the tag of hero'.

'This game is about the players, it is they who should be having their pictures in the papers. I don't like getting too much attention.'

That was obvious from his past life in Canada, Bermuda and America, but not here in Scotland. Not from the man who had courted trouble and controversy from day one at Celtic Park. The same man who was embarking on a collision course over the delayed registration at Celtic of Portuguese striker Jorge Cadete – a bitter and somewhat personal fight against the SFA and its chief executive Jim Farry which was to span the next two years.

'It is a problem not being anonymous,' he told journalists. 'I cannot use public transport, I cannot drive alone. I need security all the time.' He had hired a former Strathclyde Police detective to drive him around, picking him up at his plush Southside home and taking him back there after a day at the 'office'.

McCann continued: 'I cannot allow myself to get into the situation where I am in the midst of a group of people who are anti-Celtic and who have had a few drinks. There have been times when I have thought about giving it up because the aggro is just so great. I would like to get the chance to play golf and have time for my family.'

Meantime, there was that fight with the SFA and Farry, along with a few others. McCann was still at odds with the SFA over the insistence that Hampden Park remained the national stadium and millions be spent to ensure it did so. The Celtic boss believed it to be a white elephant and that national games could easily be accommodated at both Celtic's and Rangers' grounds.

There was also the matter of the FIFA inquiry into the legitimacy of the agents used in the transfer of Alan Stubbs to Celtic from Bolton and the claim by McCann that Monaco – a non-European Union country – should be made to pay £3 million compensation for luring Scotland international John Collins from Celtic.

Monaco got Collins for nothing, thanks to the Bosman ruling. But McCann maintained that, as a principality, Monaco was not a member of the EU and therefore fell outside the terms of the ruling. Both UEFA and FIFA said Celtic did not have a case, but McCann was still determined to pursue it and looked at all avenues of appeal. He was also facing problems of a contractual nature with Dutch striker Pierre Van Hooijdonk.

The big Dutchman was in a huff over claims that he wasn't getting the wage rise he expected. Pierre said he had an agreement that his cash would go up substantially if he produced the goods, and he had been scoring well. But McCann didn't see it that way.

It was, it appeared, a matter of dispute between McCann and the player's agent Rob Jansen who insisted that, after negotiating Pierre's transfer from Breda to Celtic, he had come to a 'verbal agreement' with McCann that the player's wages would be reviewed based on his performance.

McCann denied he had entered any such gentleman's agreement, and said a contract had been signed which included all aspects of the player's benefits from wages and bonuses right down to the number of flights back to Holland he would get from the club.

McCann was in no mood to offer a penny more for a player whose contract was due for renewal soon. If the striker wanted more money, he would have to renegotiate an extension to his commitment to Celtic and that was something he seemed reluctant to do. Too many foreign players came to Scotland on big transfers only to show their talent in the UK shop window and move on to English Premier clubs before paying back the investment in them.

Unfortunately, the man caught in the middle – once more – was manager Tommy Burns. It was becoming increasingly clear that his influence over his stars and the responsibility granted him by McCann was diminishing.

Celtic were now approaching the end of the year and looking at being unable to stop their fiercest rivals Rangers from equalling the Parkhead club's record nine-in-a-row championships. Failure to stop that happening would have its own dire consequences as Burns was only too well aware. The spirit of goodwill to all men at Celtic was now becoming a joke.

There was no doubt that Tommy Burns was one of the great Celtic supporters as well as one of the greatest servants of the club, but harsh realities as manager were now beginning to rub even harder on his weary shoulders.

He was feeling the pain of failure as much as anyone whose heart belonged to Celtic, but the job and the portfolio he inherited was a sad one. When he took over the reins at Celtic, the club had not won a trophy for five years and had gone through four managers in nine years. A sad statistic for a club which had boasted only four managers in the previous 90 years.

The manner in which McCann had gone about appointing Burns after, apparently, looking at other preferred candidates, had not helped.

For the first time in the past eight seasons, Celtic were now pushing Old Firm rivals Rangers to the limit but the task of stopping the Ibrox team equalling the nine-in-a-row feat was almost impossible now.

The pressure placed on Burns to prevent that record achievement was immense – and it was showing.

Burns had previously been quoted regarding the difference between his outlook and that of McCann. He said then: 'In Fergus's world there have to be two columns in the ledger, which are profit and loss. In mine the columns read hopes and dreams.'

There was no stopping Rangers that season as the men in blue surged to the same record already achieved and held so dearly by Celtic: nine championships in a row. The bigger task facing the Parkhead outfit as the season drew to a close was to stop the other half of the Old Firm from achieving a world record ten-in-a-row the next season. That would not be an easy task for Burns or the Celtic team he had managed to scrape together.

What didn't help morale was the attack by McCann on the discipline record of the Celtic players who strived so hard through the many difficulties to attain their best during the season.

The Hoops had a shocking total of 12 red cards over that period – the worst in Scottish football that season – and McCann didn't waste any time pointing it out to Burns.

McCann's words were well chosen to make the biggest impact and pave the way for more pressure to be heaped on Burns. The Celtic chief executive said: 'I am extremely unhappy with that record. It has been costly to the club and I do not think you can blame referees for that. It has to be laid at our own door.'

McCann seemed to have the hammer and nails for

Burns' coffin already in his hands as he added: 'I would have to say that the manager is responsible in a way. I wouldn't like to criticise the manager, but some of the judgements he has made are difficult if you look at some of the things the players have done on and off the field.

'In this day and age, unless you have a good organisation and a good, financially strong company, you will not have the results on the field.'

Strong words, but not of the supportive type that the manager of a top club would want or expect at such a crucial stage of the club's development. And it was not to stop there.

EIGHT

Bust-Up

THE new year of 1997 brought its own new problems for Celtic on top of an already full sack of old ones. The war of words between McCann and the SFA was reaching new heights, particularly over the Jorge Cadete affair.

McCann accused the overlords of Scottish football, the men who formed the committees at the SFA and were considered Jim Farry's bosses, of failure over their dealings with their chief executive.

McCann had instructed a letter to be sent to the SFA accusing Farry of misleading the public and damaging Scottish football. The Celtic supremo had even tried to sway the opinion of the SFA 'faceless' hierarchy by saying: 'Celtic has no disagreement regarding the SFA procedure. But the concern is with the damage to both Celtic, and Scottish football in general, brought about by the mishandling of Cadete's registration and recent unacceptable public statements by a senior employee of the SFA.

'With all these issues we should not have required a complaint by Celtic before being dealt with. There appears to be a reluctance to deal with the underlying problem.'

The SFA committee men publicly backed their own man and warned that Celtic may be treading on dangerous ground – words which were later to come back to haunt them.

Bill Dickie, SFA President and chairman of the executive committee, added a further threat: 'I find it sad that Celtic have gone down this route and they should realise that, if pushed, we will take a stance on such matters. Celtic seem to take an interest in everything in Scottish football and we have certainly had more letters from them than any other club.'

McCann was then embarking on a crusade which he would eventually win, but there were other cases over which he would struggle and stumble.

The temperamental Dutchman Pierre Van Hooijdonk was one of them. His contract saga with McCann ended when he left to join Nottingham Forest.

The attention then turned to Jorge Cadete who was reported to want to leave Celtic because he had 'been treated like a dog' – an allegation strongly denied by McCann.

It led the Celtic chief executive to turn once more to the media in his quest to tell his side of the story.

He said: 'I was disappointed to read the article in relation to Jorge and Celtic which was untruthful in several aspects and was published without any attempt at verification with any official with the club.

'Jorge signed a three-year deal only last year. However, in recognition of Jorge's offer to extend his contract and his exceptional form this season, Celtic have offered to extend his contract and increase his remuneration accordingly. Discussions are ongoing with Jorge's agent with a view to achieving a deal which will meet the satisfaction of all parties involved.'

It was not to be, and Cadete – who topped the Scottish goal-scoring charts that season with 28 hits – fled back to Portugal in the summer.

If that wasn't bad enough, the Celtic fans then rounded on McCann and blasted him over a snub to Parkhead favourite Paul McStay.

The storm blew up as the 1997 season drew to a close when *Evening Times* journalist John Kerr reported that McCann had failed to make the Celtic captain a new contract offer.

The fans were furious. Their comments included: 'McCann did a good job when he first came here and helping to create a new stadium but it's time he went. This is the penny-pinching mentality that we saw under the old board. We don't want a repeat of that.'

Another added: 'McCann is causing too much trouble and too much unrest. Even manager Tommy Burns doesn't know if his future is secure, and McCann isn't allowing him the authority a manager should have.'

The comments reported at the time also included this from a life-long Celtic supporter: 'McCann has messed up, interfering with the players and their contracts. He is destroying the backbone of the team. Paul is a Parkhead legend and his ability is second to none.' Despite the protestations, McStay quickly became history at Celtic Football Club.

The same newspaper then reported that the 'roller-coaster ride' of the Celtic revolution had spiralled into new and dangerous territory. It added: 'For three years under the stewardship of Fergus McCann the Parkhead club has been playing catch-up to Rangers.

'After another season in which the club has failed to wrest the championship from Ibrox, unrest at Celtic Park once again looks to be endangering the progress.

'Contractual disputes with key players, uncertainty over the future of the management and staff and a series of rows and court actions are now threatening to suffocate the life out of a club which has only recently been resuscitated from the brink of extinction.'

And yet more media speak. Another article read: 'After three years in charge at Glasgow's other half of the Old Firm, Fergus McCann has seen a sharp change in fortune.

Though they hoped for miracles, the Celtic support did not wholly expect to see them. As an unsatisfactory season draws to an anti-climactic close and McCann suddenly finds himself being scrutinised as the source of the failure.'

Brian Dempsey, the man who had paved the way for McCann to takeover at Celtic, then entered the fray much to McCann's displeasure. Dempsey was contacted while on business in the Caribbean and decided it was time to speak out. He had given McCann the time to prove his Celtic connection but it was obvious that the supporters were turning.

Dempsey said: 'I am afraid of Celtic falling into the hands of corporate interests and I want to ensure that no further damage is done to the club. I am speaking to other people and we are ready to move if we are wanted.

'I told Fergus when he came over from Canada that he could have 99 per cent of the club and still own nothing if he did not have the goodwill of the people who support Celtic.

'I would argue that Fergus has been as much misunderstood as misguided over the years but my concern is that he is consumed by his five-year business plan and lost his sense of what Celtic stands for and where it has come from.

'I don't want to see the day when Celtic fans are concerned with the club's standing on the stock market, troubled that a share deal could change everything about their team.'

Reflecting on those comments, Dempsey, who is still one of the major sponsors at the club, said: 'I clearly recall telling the other investors at the takeover about the days which would follow Fergus's return across the Atlantic.

'I told them then that when Fergus left the club he would be escaping to the anonymity of Canada or Bermuda while we, on the other hand, would be back in Glasgow and be held responsible to the community for our actions from there in.

'The club belongs to the people who saved it. Not to Fergus or the highest bidder for his shares.'

But the biggest shock to the already frail system of the Celtic support was only days away. Manager Tommy Burns, the man McCann had personally sought – albeit after looking at other candidates – was sacked.

The repercussions were fast and furious. Rangers had won the nine titles in a row, equalling Celtic's success, which every Celtic fan had dreaded. Now the man they saw as favourite to stop their rival team winning the elusive ten-in-a-row was out the door. Booted out by McCann.

More than 2,000 angry fans demonstrated outside Celtic Park after the sacking. Burns was escorted out of the stadium by four policemen only minutes after the chants from the crowd had grown into a loud condemnation of McCann. They shouted: 'Fergus, Fergus what's the score?' But no one answered until Burns came out looking distraught. Celtic public relations manager Peter McLean was left to read an announcement to the press.

It said, in the words of McCann: 'It is with regret that I announce that Celtic has decided to release Tommy Burns from the remainder of his contract. Tommy will leave immediately, but we will discuss with him our future plans and we hope he will be able to assist the club in a consultancy assignment as we make the transition to a new football–management structure.'

The Celtic chief executive tried to hide his embarrassment by saying that Burns had been offered an alternative job – looking after the youngsters at Celtic Park.

McCann said: 'Tommy Burns is a man I have a lot of respect for. That's why we offered him the opportunity to mastermind a considerable youth-development programme that would be a developed model of the system at Juventus and Ajax.'

Neither the fans nor Tommy Burns gave any credence to his comments, especially after top European players' agent

Rob Jansen labelled McCann 'the most difficult man in world football'. He added: 'Fergus McCann is the most difficult man I have ever dealt with in the world. Agents everywhere have heard about him and try hard not to have any dealings with him.'

Burns said nothing at the time, holding his head high and refusing to get involved in a slagging match with McCann, despite the urge to do so.

Another season, another disaster under McCann. Trouble was indeed brewing at Celtic Park, and more was on the way.

THERE was another departure from Celtic Park as McCann continued to fall out with those around him.

This time it was director Willie Haughey. The Glasgow millionaire businessman was blamed by McCann for leaking information about the pending departure of Burns. But Haughey had nothing to do with the stories which appeared at the time.

At first McCann denied he had sacked Haughey, claiming he had resigned.

The blow came out of the blue for Haughey. After McCann's announcement, the former director denied he had quit. He said it was up to Celtic to dismiss him, but he wasn't for going. But again there was no way back as McCann pressed his authority.

The manner in which Haughey was dismissed was shocking. Haughey was stunned. He said: 'I got a visit from Fergus McCann and Kevin Sweeney, Celtic's lawyer. They came to my office. Fergus said that, on his wishes and those of the plc board and in light of information they had received, they no longer wanted me on board. I was found guilty and convicted without any explanation. I asked him why, but he refused to give me any details.

'I was given the option of resigning, but I said no. While talking to them I heard that Celtic's public relations department was already putting the story out that I had resigned and telling journalists that, off the record, it was because I had leaked information to the press.

'When I heard this I told them to stop all talks about any resignation. All bets were off. Then I lambasted Fergus McCann. It was a cowardly way for the club and McCann to behave. I remember the day clearly. I was sitting in my office just after 5 p.m. when I got a telephone call through to my secretary asking if Mr McCann could pop in and see me – which he'd done on two or three occasions in the past few years and didn't seem any big deal.

'About 15 minutes later I went to the reception and he was there along with Kevin Sweeney who was the secretary of the plc, and we went into my office. Basically, he said to me that it wasn't a nice task they were there for.

'That was his opening line. McCann then said: "Before I tell you what it is, I can tell you I will not be answering any questions at all." He said he had the backing of the plc board to remove me from from the board. I just laughed. I thought he was joking. I looked at Kevin Sweeney who confirmed it.

'I asked him what the charges were, but he didn't tell me: He simply said if I wanted to resign they could put out the right wording. It was left at that, and Kevin Sweeney said if I wanted to get my lawyer to phone him up at the Park then just do so.

'I was sitting racking my brain, thinking: "What have I done?" I couldn't come up with anything and probably, until this day, would have had no idea until, right out of the blue, I got a phone call from a journalist who was in Sweden at Scotland's World Cup qualifier.

'I was in Glasgow at the time the journalist called. He

said that someone from Celtic had phoned and told a fellow journalist that I had just resigned, but if I hadn't then it was only a matter of time because they were going to sack me for leaking a story to the press.

'It was all innuendo, and I told Fergus that in front of TV cameras. He said publicly he didn't want to say what the crime was and he said it was in my interests and the club's interests not to say. I told him it wasn't in *my* interests. I would be delighted if he wanted to tell the world what I had supposedly done. That has never been done to this day.

'I feel that I have completely vindicated myself. I don't know if you've seen this, but they put a press release out in *The Celtic View*, because I persuaded them to come clean. They actually put a statement in the *Celtic View* to say that I had nothing whatsoever to do with leaks from Celtic Football Club and that the reason I was going was due to differences of opinion with the chairman.

'That was important. I wanted to make sure that the Celtic fans knew there what the truth was. It was typical of Fergus. A lot of the time we didn't even know what was going on at the club even though we were directors.

'To be fair, I think that was a good thing sometimes, not knowing until later. There might have been some things that frustrate you, but that happens in every board – but the things that we used to find out late were wee daft things, not to do with the football, things like Celtic Insurance Services.'

But one thing which did frustrate and annoy Willie Haughey was the promise from McCann that he would back the former director's dream of creating a youth soccer academy, similar to that which has brought forward generations of new young and promising players at Juventus and Ajax.

But it was a pipe dream fed to Haughey. He said: 'It was something that could have been done, and something I would like to have pursued. It didn't happen because at that time our relationship with the SFA was not at its best and also Celtic had to have clearance from them to make the move. So I think that it froze.'

Talking about the SFA and McCann's attitude to the sports overlords, Haughey said: 'I think on some of the occasions he was right. I thought the fine for the Kilmarnock issue was absolutely diabolical, but I think with a bit of commonsense some of the things could have been done a little bit better.'

Then he spoke about an incredible plan to buy over Wimbledon Football Club and have Celtic join the English Premier League.

He said: 'I'm not saying it would be quite easy, but it was something that could have been progressed, and suddenly you are taking Celtic into another and bigger field of play – you know, it's a whole new world – commercially it's £10 million for being in the premier league – but only if we go into that league as Celtic.

'We could have got away with just changing the venue. We only had to apply for a change of venue. There would probably be opposition, but it could be done. You go to teams like Brighton and all those other teams that are bottom of the league but they have 100 years of history then maybe you wouldn't be able to pull it off. But Wimbledon had 3,000 at Selhurst Park. That's not much opposition is it?

'I tried to pursue it, but to get it right was really difficult. It was never discussed in detail. It was all my own research. It was a notion, but an achievable one. I would like to think it would have been worth pursuing. Some of the other things we did pursue and got nowhere, but this could have been a big, big win if it had gone through.'

When Haughey was ousted, the men at the helm of the football board at Celtic consisted of McCann, Michael McDonald, Eric Riley, David Kells, Dominic Keane and

John Keane. The plc governing board had McCann, Riley, Brian Quinn, Dermot Desmond and Sir Patrick Sheehy. David Kells and company secretary Kevin Sweeney became directors later.

Haughey's friends on the board were Dominic Keane and Michael McDonald. After the news of Haughey's departure, McDonald, who was on business in Manchester, drove back to Glasgow and said: 'I have spoken to both Fergus and Willie but, until I find out exactly what's going on, I won't comment further. Willie is a personal friend, and I'm obviously disappointed with what's happened. Once I have attended the board meeting that has been called, I may have more to say.'

Dominic Keane did have more to say, but he wanted to say it to Fergus's face first before speaking to the media in any great detail.

Keane lambasted McCann and then followed his friend Haughey out of the door. He quit.

The man, who along with his tax-exile brother Eddie, had fought long and hard to help McCann gain power, now said he had had enough.

He added: 'Resigning from Celtic was the hardest thing I have ever done, but I felt it was the right thing to do. There was no evidence offered to prove any case against Willie, and I personally believe he is not to blame for what is being said.

'Principle was the most important thing here. It hurts, but it had to be done. I wish the club success.'

Haughey was full of admiration for the stand made by Keane, saying: 'It is quite unbelievable what Dominic has done because I know how much that club means to him and what being a director meant to him. I can't really put it into words. I spoke to Dominic on the telephone, but he was too distraught to say much.

'I feel worse for him than for myself, but it all highlights the sort of problems the club faces off the park.'

McCann said: 'I understand Dominic Keane was not in agreement with the process by which Mr Haughey had to be removed. However, the board support my position, as managing director and majority shareholder, that it is in the best interests of all parties, including Mr Haughey, that the specific reasons for that decision remain confidential to those who made it. Dominic has assured me he knows that I and my colleagues will continue to do what we believe is right to take Celtic forward, and I appreciate that.'

Looking back on the days which stunned him, Haughey and Celtic, as well as the fans, Keane said: 'During the last year or 18 months that I was on the board, a mistrust developed. You know, people like Willie, who'd been great supporters, and myself, we felt it. We were conscious that the last thing we wanted to do was to destabilise the regime by speaking out because there was a lot of hard work done to achieve the changes at Celtic and a lot of Celtic supporters had put trust in those who were on the board.

'In the early days we'd gone out and sold this share issue. We'd sold the vision, we'd sold the dream. Therefore, nearly six months after taking the Celtic supporters' money, for us to come out and say we've fallen out or we can't agree over this and that, I think would've been bad for the club at that time. So we dug in and we endeavoured to change things around.

'We tried to influence the decision making at board level, but there were lots of things that went on in the background that we were never aware of. You know a good example, a classic example was that, as the club got stronger and stronger financially, the need for the football board was becoming – in my view – less and less. Having said that and to be fair, if we asked a question we would get answers, but you can't be expected at every board meeting to always have to ask and ask in order to find out what was going on.

'I think there was a deep mistrust among the different

players within the new board, and I think that was borne out by the fact that Fergus was becoming more and more autocratic in his style of management. He'd probably disagree with that, but I think he was – and I would have said that in the early days. I was in there virtually all the time, so I saw it. I did the financial director's job for the first period, I did the secretary's job, I did the administration and I carried out the commercial work for a period after Patrick Ferrell leaving. I was party to a lot of things. I was probably the closest person to Fergus in the first two years of the regime.

'In the early days you certainly could go in and have a chat with him and, overall, he would give you the time. He would listen. He wouldn't always agree with you, but he would listen. However, all of that began to change. I think in the last year or so when I was there – whether it was because of the pressure he found himself under – I found it more difficult to converse with him.

'He would become much more agitated, much more frustrated – especially after his relationship with Tommy Burns had reached the level where it was clear that Tommy wasn't a long-term prospect.

'Fergus didn't have any great feelings for the football department at all by this time and he interfered a lot. There was virtually nothing going on in the football department that he didn't want to know about. I remember Tommy Burns once asking for a fax machine in his office and he was told that wasn't a possibility. All the faxes had to come up through secretariat, and I believe that was because Fergus wanted to know everything that was coming in about players, everything about the problems with the contracts which were emerging at this time, you know, Pierre Van Hooijdonk and Jorge Cadete. There were a lot of things going on in the background, and it was becoming clear to certain members of the board that we, as directors, were becoming less important. We would always be given the time of day, we would always be given our seat in the stand, we would always be at a board meeting and all the background papers would be there, but there were clearly major issues in the background.

'It got to the stage where most people kept out of his way. It was easier for me because I wasn't a paid employee. I was there to be secretary for the administration and football side, and I could see people would keep out his way.

'After a while there was only one way to do things, and that was to do it Fergus's way – no matter what he would say and what other people would say. I was in there every day and I saw the people take the easy option, the one that Fergus wanted. Now that didn't happen every time at the club, but where he had an influence or an opinion that was what Fergus wanted. He was a difficult man to convince otherwise, and there were not an awful lot of people who I would describe as having the character to oppose him.

'That was why the board with Willie Haughey and the other non-executive directors such as John Keane, Michael McDonald and myself were important. We weren't paid employees and we weren't easily bossed. We were there to oversee – principally on the football side – that things were being run along the lines of the promises which were made to the supporters and people who put their millions of pounds into Celtic buying shares and season-tickets. Therefore, it was easier for us to sit at a board meeting and argue on a whole range of issues.'

ONE of the major issues was that of Tommy Burns and the circumstances surrounding his working relationship with McCann and his eventual departure.

Keane recalled: 'I think Fergus had lost total confidence in Tommy after the Scottish Cup final victory when Tommy made it clear that he was probably going to leave – there were hastily convened meetings which are well documented and it was probably Willie Haughey's intervention, which I think was the right thing at the time, which saved things.

'We had just won the Scottish Cup and the last thing we wanted was to lose the manager who had won the first trophy in about six or seven years. Fergus, in my view, accepted the compromise of a letter of apology from Tommy Burns which was very carefully worded and basically written by Willie Haughey. Willie convinced both Fergus and Tommy that this compromise should be in the best interests of Celtic at that time. But I think it was evident then that Tommy would have a real difficult run in over the next year or two because, in my opinion, Fergus is someone who doesn't easily forget things or people which upset him.

'Going back to the Kilmarnock affair, I'm not sure it would be right to suggest that Fergus wanted Tommy Burns to tell lies – you couldn't say for sure that was the case. I think Fergus's interpretation of tapping was clearly different from Tommy's, and I think it became evident that we were being victimised by the SFA over the Tommy Burns affair. I am sure that that type of third-party discussion – which tapping is – goes on all the time in football, but I think, looking back, perhaps we should have accepted that yes, we did use a third party to bring about the appointment of Tommy Burns.

'If we had accepted that and admitted it then, much of the bad publicity that surrounded us around that time and all the bad will that was created between ourselves and other members of the football fraternity and other regulatory bodies could have been avoided. Perhaps the level of fine imposed would have been much less had we sat down and just negotiated – accepted that we had inadvertently strayed on to the wrong side – maybe if we had taken the more apologetic route, that, yes, we had spoken to Tommy Burns through a third party and we were sorry that this should have happened then much of the bad blood would not be there.

'But Fergus's tactics were much more aggressive and, I think, being new to football, he tried to take on the establishment too early. I think that affair soured, at the very early stages, his relationship with Tommy. Things didn't really improve during that first season and there were numerous examples of fall-outs between himself and Tommy. He felt that Tommy was somebody who was a bit headstrong, far too headstrong. Fergus wanted total control and he found it difficult to control Tommy. Tommy was taking on more and more responsibility – he tried at a very early stage to right all the wrong and he felt all the pressure of all those years with Celtic had meant nothing. He was trying to build the football department – probably too quickly – and it was clear he took on too much. You know coaches nowadays, Venglos and Wim Jansen, they look after the first team and the first team only. Tommy Burns rebuilt the youth and the reserves, handled the first team, had to go out and look at players, went to all the functions – sometimes he was going to two functions a night – and he just became a complete and utter workaholic to such an extent it was probably impossible for him to concentrate on his main role, which was to produce a team which was capable at that time of winning the league and stopping the Rangers win which equalled our nine-in-a-row.

'We looked at setting up this footballing committee to ease the pressure on Tommy, but it would never have worked and, anyway, Fergus had made up his own mind at the end of the day and knew how things were going to be done. So within eight or nine months of Tommy being there, the relationship between the two was very, very difficult and that put pressure on the board as well. It was clear that we were all so ambitious, but if your chief executive and your football coach don't have a relationship, that's a problem. I don't care what kind of business you're in, that's a major problem. So although we muddled through that year playing at Hampden while Celtic Park was being rebuilt, it was a very difficult year for Tommy Burns – although we ended up with the Scottish Cup at the end of the season.

'Then we went into the sixth season at Celtic Park and although we got off to a bad start, we lost a game against Rangers, Tommy Burns's record that year was exceptional. He lost one league game. What became clear to us was that Tommy was gaining a lot of respect and, although he failed to win a domestic trophy that season, his team was gaining a lot of plaudits. But the friction between him and Fergus was never smoothed over, and it was always the case that Tommy would feel vulnerable, isolated, but there was nothing during that year to suggest the relationship between him and Fergus was even at the lower end of what is acceptable in any business. We all tried at different times in the season to try and help the situation when Tommy was at the meetings but whether we were helping or hindering, I am not really sure.

'We felt that the team was gaining respect, playing good football and the supporters were enjoying coming to Celtic, to what was the revamped Celtic Park. Then, around that time, the Boys' Club affair was breaking and that was another major source of accusation between Celtic plc and Tommy Burns, because of Tommy's relationship and strength of feeling and admiration and closeness to Frank Cairney who was accused of certain things along with Jim Torbett.

'Although I'm not overly versed on events regarding Cairney and the Boys' Club, because I didn't know much about the Boys' Club, this was another major area of fall-out between Fergus and Tommy Burns.

'McCann just didn't like Tommy having Frank Cairney around at all. So against all that background we moved into his third year, which was his last year. And there was no doubt in Fergus's mind that Tommy wasn't getting a new contract. So apart from the pressure of trying to stop nine in a row now, that season became one of the worst seasons in history so far as Celtic and our record against Rangers was concerned.

'I think that during that year there was an atmosphere which existed between both the clubs and the supporters and was built up by the media because of the significance of nine in a row. So when you look at Tommy Burns, he was coming to the end of his contract, under pressure to deliver a title, had a very poor relationship with Fergus, which by that time was practically non-existent, feeling that he wasn't getting as many resources as he could for the team and problems were beginning to emerge with contractual situations, Pierre in particular. It was clear that Tommy Burns was beginning to feel the strain.

'Going into the third year of a pressure-pot situation, working under Fergus, he was beginning to find it very difficult. I didn't know Tommy Burns prior to him becoming Celtic's manager, I didn't know him well, but it was plain that Tommy Burns in that last year was suffering from the strains and pressures – some of which he brought on himself – but mostly through working under the regime at that time. To be fair, I was part of that and probably as guilty as anyone of putting him under pressure to win the league.

'I think that pressure led to him making some irrational decisions with the team, and he found it difficult to understand where Fergus was coming from. I think he felt it was his last year and, even if he won the League or Cup, Fergus would be looking to change the structure anyway. So probably by the turn of the year, Tommy felt his days were numbered.'

ACCORDING to Dominic Keane it was not just Tommy Burns who was involved in clashes with McCann at that stage.

He said: 'Willie Haughey and Fergus were entering into exchanges of correspondence by the turn of that year on a whole range of issues where Willie felt that the club was not acting in a manner which he felt was the proper way for Celtic. These were private issues, which were confidential to the board and, therefore, although I can't disclose the exact nature of them, I can tell you they were fundamental issues concerning the way Celtic should be run and the way in which supporters should be treated. It got to the stage that Willie found it difficult to converse with Fergus and vice versa, so the only way they could do it was by entering into correspondence.

'I can only surmise that Fergus took the bull by the horns and decided that he'd had enough of Willie and felt he couldn't work with him any longer. So when he arrived down at Willie's office that night with Kevin Sweeney, he effectively asked Willie to resign and subsequently dismissed him. You know, he did it in such a way that, in my view, he had no basic right to. He hadn't consulted anybody. He said he had consulted the plc board, but what did he consult them with? What information did he have? The fact is, he didn't have any information. He decided that because somebody within Celtic Park was prepared to stand up to him on issues which were fundamental to the rights of the supporters then he found that he just couldn't live with it any longer. He'd had enough of that.

'They were issues that were to do with the way in which Celtic had relationships with the supporters' associations, and there were also other issues internally in the way in which the club was being run and how information was being passed down on several matters that have never come out. Unfortunately, they can't come out from us because it would be a breach of confidentiality.

'They were issues sometimes small, sometimes major, and it could go back as far as the Celtic Insurance Services. The board were warned. So when Fergus and Kevin Sweeney removed Willie that night I got home and I had two phone calls, one from Willie and one from Fergus. Willie said that he'd been sacked and I couldn't believe it. Then I phoned Fergus and he said not to speak to anybody or give any statements out, it would all be explained at a board meeting the next day. Although I was, to a certain extent, friendly with Fergus, I knew not to be influenced by anything that he said and that there was more to this than met the eye. So the next day there was a board meeting and some of the issues we were going to discuss that day were Tommy Burns and creating a new structure to help him – including talking about a General Manager and coach – things to take us into the twenty-first century. Now Willie's sacking was top of the agenda. Fergus had phoned us again that morning and told us not to speak to anybody and that if anybody from the press phoned we couldn't speak to them because we were not empowered to.

'Prior to that meeting I went up and met with Willie and said I was going as I didn't think that I would be there that long because if he could do that to him then he could do it to anyone else. I also asked if there was anything I should know about and he showed me the correspondence between him and McCann, all of which I felt were things that had been raised at board meetings and were valid issues which he wasn't getting any answers to. He had been quite right to challenge the issues – these were issues we, as board members, were there to ensure were dealt with in order to fulfil our responsibilities. I drove down to the Park and the phone rang and Fergus said: "I hope you haven't spoken to anybody. I hope you haven't spoken to any press." I told him I hadn't spoken to anybody. He said "Right, we are expecting a bit of trouble here today. We are expecting that Willie might appear at this meeting."

'I said I didn't think so. I turned up at the front door and Celtic's security guy, George Douglas, was there and there were other security present. I couldn't believe that three and a half years on from that euphoric evening when we threw out the old board we once again had Fortress Celtic, and I said that to George Douglas. He said it was in case Willie appeared and I said: "What would you do if he did appear?" I never got an answer to that. I said to George: "God, what have we come to in this place when we've got additional security presence on to stop a man who has been nothing but the most supportive guy in the three and a half years that I've been in here?" When the share issue was falling apart at the seams, he was the guy who resurrected it by convincing Gerald Weisfeld, John Keane and my brother Eddie to put money up to match the Dermott Desmond injection of money for shares. I went through the doors and into the boardroom. They were just convening and the first thing I said to Fergus was, "Fergus, what the hell is going on here?" He also said it was just in case Willie appeared and again I asked: "What the hell would you have done? What would we have done? Thrown him out? Have him arrested?" I said to Fergus that was what we had fought to change here and what about the open-door policy he'd promised when he told the press "My door will always be open"?

'So, without saying too much about the board meeting, I think it's fair to say that Fergus just expected that the members of the football board – John Keane Mike McDonald, Eric Reilly and Kevin Sweeney – would accept

Fergus's explanation that it was in the best interests of the club for Willie to be no longer part of the board and that he had information to that effect. But I challenged him and I asked what information he did have regarding Willie Haughey and, of course, he didn't have any.

'Most of us knew exactly what was happening. We knew about the exchange of correspondence. We knew that Willie was becoming more and more like Tommy and the rest of us – becoming frustrated that it was Fergus's way or no way at all.

'You know, I think that probably Willie would have become so frustrated and upset at the lack of answers that he probably would have left anyway to get on with his own business and become just an ambassador of the club again. I think he felt he just couldn't work with Fergus and the way he was running the operation any longer. But that was not the issue right there and then at that board meeting, and I objected. Fergus more or less asked us just to accept the fact and that that was the way it was going to be, but I said: "Oh no, we won't, we can't accept that." His attitude then was to get on with the items on the agenda; he didn't want to talk about this any more. I didn't have the backing. At the end of the meeting I raised the issue again because I thought it was disgraceful to treat people like this. I told him I thought Willie should be brought back and that you shouldn't treat people like that. Fergus said: "Look, we will just leave this, I am not going to talk about it any more." And he walked out. The rest of the meeting was about Tommy Burns that day but, quite frankly, I think it was overshadowed by the removal of Willie Haughey.

'I went home that night and I spoke to my wife and we talked things through. I spoke to a lot of people, my closest friends, and I spoke to Willie who told me not to resign as that is what they wanted, what Fergus wanted. But I had made up my mind I wanted to leave and I decided I wanted to see McCann the next day.

'It took me a long time to prepare my letter, word it carefully and explain why I was coming to the decision I was, because it was one of the hardest decisions I had ever made in my life. That's probably because it's Celtic. The next afternoon I got a phone call from Fergus asking if I could pop up to his office because he had something he wanted to talk to me about.

'He said he thought thought that we could have a chat to Tommy about this youth development project. What he was trying to do was win me back over so that I was part of the new team and to forget about Willie. Fergus said to me: "You and I can work together, and you're very important to Celtic going forward and you and I can talk to Tommy. Maybe the strain's been too much for him, so we'll talk about offering him a post as head of youth development or something."

'I told him I didn't even want to think about that discussion. I only had one thing on my mind and that was for him to tell me the truth about Willie.

'I said: "Fergus, you cannot operate this business the way you are running it just now. You can't continue to treat people the way you are treating them. People like Willie Haughey are some of the strongest supporters of what you tried to achieve during those early years – he could have brought you down before we were even entrenched in that EGM in May of 1995, but he supported the new regime throughout that period on every single major issue.

'Willie Haughey, as did all of us, stood shoulder to shoulder with you. Clearly there were other times when we had disagreements but not to the extent where you could decide without any consultation and without giving anybody apart from your closest allies on that board information as to why you could arrive at the decision you arrived at."

'At that point Fergus banged the table with his fist. He said: "That is the matter closed!" I leaned forward and I banged the desk back and I told him: "Don't you ever talk to me in that tone again!"

'At that point I think he realised that he had overstepped the way in which he could talk to me. I told him I couldn't work as part of his team anymore. I told him I didn't want to leave but he'd given me no choice – not when he had single-handedly removed a director and not told the other directors why or consulted them in advance. I couldn't care what business we were in, it just wasn't acceptable.

'He asked me not to resign but I said: "Fergus you can't be part of what we have done in the past three and a half years and not have respect for one another but, at the same time, you've got to understand that this is not just your club, this is also the club of 60,000 people. You cannot just run it the way you want. You've got to listen to other people. Sure, some hard decisions have got to be made and the buck always stops with the chief executive, but you have got to listen to other people who also care about the place."

'At that point he tried to get Eric Reilly to change my mind. When that failed he brought in David Kells. David was somebody I had worked with at the time when he had become a director. I was a bit emotional when I left my letter with Eric and I asked him to read it out to the others.

'I knew I had done the right thing. And when I walked out that door, I don't think I could ever feel the way I felt then. I went to see Willie and I told him what I had done. He thought I should maybe have stayed in and fought our corner. It was one of the worst days of my life but I just couldn't be part of that regime. How could I get up in the morning and look at myself in the mirror? I couldn't have done that so I walked.'

One man who wasn't for walking was McCann. Many of the fans were calling for him to go but, despite the outcry over Haughey and Keane, he told journalists: 'I'll go when I am ready to go and not before.'

NINE

Dirty Washing

CELTIC, under Fergus McCann, astounded their fans, as well as the media and the rest of Scottish Football, with one big shock signing shortly after removing manager Tommy Burns.

It was not a player who caused the gasps of disbelief, it was the appointment of part-time lawyer and television football commentator Jock Brown, brother of Scotland manager Craig.

He was hired to the new post of general manager at the club – a post identified as a way of taking pressure off the manager who could now concentrate on the team under another new title: coach. The trouble was that Celtic was still without a team leader whether he be a manager or a coach. And there was no candidate in sight to replace Burns, although McCann was reported to have held talks with Dutchman Wim Jansen on the very day Brown was appointed.

Jansen, a former Dutch internationalist and Feyenoord coach, was later to accept the post after becoming one of Brown's first tasks on the negotiations front at Celtic.

Brown's other tasks of a similar nature were a little tougher – the problems over the club's two moody foreigners: Italian Paolo di Canio and Portugal's Jorge Cadete. They were two of the three controversial internationalists dubbed the 'Three Amigos' by McCann. The other, Dutchman Pierre Van Hooijdonk, had already departed to England under a cloud.

Both Cadete and di Canio were planning similar moves. The Italian was also threatening to take McCann to court over a £25,000 fine slapped on him by the managing director after he criticised McCann's methods. Cadete was upset over money he claimed he was due after his transfer from Portugal.

Both were not to last much longer at the club, and both highlighted the sort of dealings and sayings Brown was to be famous for. Di Canio was 'not for sale' on the Tuesday but 'traded' to Sheffield Wednesday on the Wednesday. More was yet to come with assistant general manager and scout, Davie Hay, a previous manager of the team, also getting booted out of Celtic. It was yet another sad departure of a man who had given a great chunk of his life to the club.

By then the new season was up and running and Celtic had to ensure that they stopped their Old Firm rivals reaching that elusive ten in a row when the league ended in the spring of 1998. That would be a disaster.

Another disaster, and one which gave Brown a sharp taste of football life on the wrong end of a tongue-lashing, came at Celtic's AGM three months after taking up his post.

Around 1,000 shareholders at the meeting in the main stand at Celtic Park launched a scathing attack on McCann – with Brown getting a share of the verbal abuse.

The fans demanded answers over the team's lack of success, the sacking of Tommy Burns and the loss of top players.

There were shouts of 'rubbish' as McCann tried to pacify the shareholders with boasts of financial success at the club. They were not interested in paper profit – only silverware was important at this proud club.

Haughey and Keane were also among the shareholders

and both took the opportunity to join the criticism. When McCann was asked why they had lost Cadete, Van Hooijdonk and Di Canio it was Brown who replied to the shareholders with the cutting remark: 'You made them stars and they got too big for their boots.' Further boos followed and when McCann attempted to boast again about the finances at the club he was again heckled. He blasted back: 'If you don't have the profits you don't have a team.' There then followed shouts of: 'Well spend the profits.' McCann and Brown both said they would but added that they would not be rushed into any quick signings.

Another fan hit out: 'You've done nothing McCann. I wouldn't believe a word you say. Why is it when players, directors and managers disagree with you they are out the door?' A rattled McCann failed to answer directly and, as the meeting became even more heated, he refused to take any more questions despite demands from the shareholders for answers – a scenario to which both Haughey and Keane could easily relate. There was the hint of a smile on the faces of the former directors as the meeting broke up in disarray.

ANOTHER fight going on in another corner of the Celtic playground was the hearing into former manager Lou Macari's sacking.

Macari was suing Celtic for £431,000 over his departure in June 1994 to make way for Tommy Burns. Celtic was counter-suing for the £250,000 it had paid to Stoke City to take Macari from his contract in October 1993 as Macari had now gone back to the club. But McCann had now instructed that an alternative claim be dropped.

The alternative claim, should the first action fail, was to pursue Macari for £150,000 – the same amount it had paid Kilmarnock for 'poaching' Burns. McCann's argument was, if Macari had not been in breach of contract, the club would have had ample time to find a successor without incurring the penalty to Kilmarnock for Burns.

That claim now had to be dropped if Celtic were to safeguard its position and not be forced to reveal what other candidates were considered or approached to replace Macari before the job eventually went to Burns.

The issue of the other candidates was first raised earlier at the Court of Session hearing in Edinburgh by counsel for Macari who wanted to know if any other candidate had been rejected by Celtic in favour of a cheaper option to bring in Burns.

McCann had been grilled in the box for five days and, through his counsel, had chosen to stick to 'confidentiality' on the issue.

His counsel told judge Lady Cosgrove that 'to reveal the names of other candidates now, by whatever means, would be extremely embarrassing to all concerned.' It was one of the few backdowns McCann had ever made. It also turned out to be one of McCann's biggest embarrassments.

He was really put through the mill over the Macari case – and Tommy Burns was there to help the man he replaced. There was no love lost between the men who had managed the club and the man who had managed to club them out.

Burns told how he wanted to put his staff at ease by telling them they had another couple of years to take the club forward but he claimed McCann had become 'evasive' and didn't want to talk about the future. He had gone into McCann's office to speak to him but it was empty. Empty, that is, except for a document lying on the table which had the name of Tommy Burns on it.

Burns said: 'It basically just caught my eye. I glanced at

it and saw my name and read through some things.' The document turned out to be board papers which had been included in confidential letters to the club's lawyers in which board members had slated Burns for the club's poor disciplinary record.

He was also blamed for being 'intense and emotional'. Burns said: 'It was saying that my relationship with the managing director had never been right and it was possibly best for a change. McCann later told me they would not be renewing my contract. It could have been handled with a lot more dignity.'

He then told of how he had started the job at a great disadvantage with Rangers having much more cash to spend on players.

Burns added: 'We had to basically start from scratch as they had a huge start on us. My need was greater than any other manager. It was very difficult to get any continuity within the club because it wasn't being run the way a normal football club should be at the time.'

McCann's former ally, Brian Dempsey, was the next to take the stand and he too was stinging in his remarks about the Celtic managing director.

Dempsey recalled how he had recommended to McCann after the takeover of the club back in 1994 that Macari should go but he revealed his shock when McCann publicly demeaned Macari in front of potential investors in the club.

The Glasgow millionaire businessman said: 'I had spoken to Mr McCann about the issues facing Celtic and one of the most prominent was, in my opinion, the manager. I recommended Mr Macari should be dismissed as, quite simply, then was the time for major change with the whole system of management and the whole ethos of the club changing. If there were any remnants from the past they would not help take the club forward. No distraction could be afforded.'

His view was that everyone in the new set-up should work together and he felt that Macari had been a supporter of the old board. Dempsey also said he had suggested Tommy Burns be approached to takeover the job and McCann told him he would go away and think over the ideas.

Dempsey added: 'Mr McCann telephoned me just before I was heading out to America for the World Cup and he told me he was taking my recommendation to dismiss Mr Macari the next day. But, at a meeting with other potential investors in the club, Mr McCann openly demeaned Mr Macari. That more than hit me because it caused me a great deal of concern that any one of us in that room would feel derogatory about the Celtic manager. I took it to be an American colloquialism which Mr McCann was given to use. I was concerned over the effect the remark could have on the standing of Celtic Football Club.'

The civil case at the Court of Session in Edinburgh was an embarrassment to both Celtic and to McCann. But, four months later, it was McCann who was smiling when Macari lost the case.

But the smile was not as wide as it could be after the managing director was labelled 'a rather devious individual' by judge Lady Cosgrove. Her 82-page judgment dismissed Macari's unfair dismissal action but the judge said she had a clear impression after hearing the evidence that McCann was 'an uncompromising and somewhat arrogant employer who expected unquestioning compliance with his instructions and unfailing deference to his views.'

She added: 'He was frequently reluctant to answer the precise question posed and I formed the impression of a rather devious individual. I formed a clear impression that Mr McCann was a somewhat uncommunicative individual with whom it was not particularly easy to establish a rapport.'

On Macari, Lady Cosgrove said: 'He impressed me as an amiable but not particularly astute individual who seemed to have failed to appreciate either the nature of the man who had become his employer or his methods. Whether through understandable anxiety about losing his job or through a stubborn or blinkered belief that the way things had been previously was right and should not be changed, particularly by a managing director who was not knowledgeable about football matters, or a combination of the two, he forced issues to the point of confrontation and put himself in clear breach of his contract.'

She also dismissed Celtic's counter-claim against Macari leaving him to pick up substantial legal bills for the whole sorry affair.

THERE was some good news to come out of Celtic Park as the club stumbled into 1998 through the off-the-field controversy. Results on the pitch were improving under new manager Wim Jansen. Things were definitely looking up.

Celtic had got off to a good start in Europe, whipping Welsh outfit Inter CableTel 8–0 over the two legs. The team then lost 2–1 to Tirol in Austria but then hammered them 6–3 at Celtic Park.

Progress was also good on the domestic front. The league charge had a faltering start but the club then booked a place in the semi-finals of the Coca-Cola Cup with a 1–0 victory over Motherwell.

Unfortunately Celtic's Euro-run came to a halt against Liverpool after a titanic struggle. The teams drew 2–2 at Parkhead and then 0–0 at Anfield with Celtic going out on the away goals rule.

But it was then off to Ibrox for the domestic cup semi-final where they beat Dunfermline 1–0 to reach the final, where they then picked up the performance to win the Cup with a 3–0 scoreline over Dundee United. The goals came from recent signings Marc Rieper and Henrik Larsson and from Craig Burley.

The Celtic fans at last approached a Christmas in good spirits, having a trophy again in the cupboard, although the team was struggling a bit in the league and trailing leaders Rangers – the team they could not afford to let win the record-breaking ten in a row.

But 1998 saw a great start with a 2–0 victory over their Old Firm rivals in the New Year derby at Celtic Park. The side then closed the gap on Rangers to three points after another goal from Craig Burley gave the team another win over Dundee United – this time by 2–1 in the league match at Tannadice while Rangers dropped points after defeat at St Johnstone. The two bitter rivals were then neck-and-neck at the top of the table with Hearts after Celtic beat Aberdeen 3–1. Rangers slipped up again drawing with Dunfermline but Celtic could only take a point from Hearts in the table-top clash at Tynecastle.

Unfortunately, and rather predictably, the attention at Celtic did not stay long on the playing field and was back on club politics. This time Jock Brown was the man drawing the flack as news broke over constant clashes between him and manager Wim Jansen. Anger again rose from the Celtic supporters as Jansen threatened to quit the club after yet another bust-up with Brown.

The backroom feud between the former television commentator and the Dutch coach was threatening to affect the team's chances of preventing Rangers taking the record league title. Jansen was said to be 'appalled' at the interference he was suffering at the hands of Brown.

The coach was unhappy with the sacking of Davie Hay and the appointment of two assistant coaches from the SFA without any reference to him. Jansen felt he was being left out of major decisions regarding the playing side. The signs were not good and McCann was once more embroiled in controversy which he himself had helped create through Brown's appointment and the subsequent power struggle between coach and general manager.

Brown attempted to play down the row between him and Jansen by speaking of his 'respect' for the coach but added: 'I'm the buffer between what happens in the boardroom and what happens on the field. It is impossible in the modern game for any one person to fulfil all the roles the former team managers used to.'

Fortunately the team didn't appear to suffer too much and, with Rangers drawing with Hearts, a Celtic win over Hibs saw the Parkhead outfit taking over top spot in the league at the end of February. But the fans were in a sweat. Off the park Jansen revealed he had a 'get-out clause' in his contract and might use it. On the park, Celtic crashed 2–1 to Rangers in the Scottish Cup semi-final and then suffered a second defeat by the Ibrox team in the league, which left the two Old Firm rivals sharing top spot once more.

Both sides dropped points but when Rangers lost to Kilmarnock at the start of May it left Celtic needing a victory over Dunfermline the very next day to clinch the championship for the first time in a decade and halt the Rangers victory train. But the Hoops blew it, drawing 1–1 at East End Park. It was then down to the final game of the season. All Celtic had to do was beat St Johnstone at Parkhead and, no matter what Rangers did, Celtic would have the Championship. They duly delivered with a 2–0 victory. A victory which was so very sweet to the faithful Celtic fans who had stuck by their team in times of crisis. But it was a victory which just as quickly turned sour when, only 48 hours later with the team in Portugal for a friendly match and a celebration break, Wim Jansen announced he was quitting. He'd had enough of Brown and the lack of support from McCann.

Once more Celtic had been plunged into chaos, ripping apart the hearts of the Celtic supporters who barely had time to bask in that long-awaited glory. The players too were stunned.

Fans marched on Celtic Park demanding the resignations of both McCann and Brown. Their fury grew when McCann announced he would have sacked Jansen anyway if he hadn't quit. The supporters were stunned. McCann said: 'I think it is almost certain that not only I, but Jock Brown and the board, felt he could not continue long term. I found there was a continued refusal on the part of Wim to accept responsibility. It was always someone else's fault, either the players' quality or Jock Brown was the problem. Wim had to fit in with the Celtic plans for the future but he was not prepared to do that.'

Speaking from a Portuguese hotel Jansen said he was dismayed. He did not deny McCann's comment about Celtic's future but added: 'I am leaving because I think I have different ideas than the people at Celtic as to how this club should go but I must say that Celtic were not as ambitious as I was. I have a different opinion from them about how you make a big club.

'My relationship with Jock Brown was bad from beginning to end. In the past few months I couldn't even speak to him. In fact I wanted to resign just two or three weeks after I took the job but they wouldn't accept it. But the team I built up will always be part of me and I leave also with many good memories.'

A full statement from Celtic on behalf of McCann soon followed. McCann said: 'This period of time is about Celtic winning the Championship and the supporters and players deserve to celebrate. As for Wim Jansen, he originally wanted a one-year contract. The club agreed a three-year term with the option for both sides to terminate the contract after one year.

'Wim has decided to leave after one year. The club accept Wim's decision, which is not unexpected. The decision Wim has taken is also one the board believes is best for the club. I would like to thank Wim and wish him all the best for the future.

'The supporters should not let Wim's decision deflect their attention and pleasure from the point that the league has been won. They deserve to celebrate. Wim has played a part and no one should deny that, but so have many others.

'Celtic has risen through adversity and has become stronger every season for the last four years. I have no doubt this will continue next season as the club moves onwards and upwards. All of this was not the result of the efforts of only one season or one man.

'I want to pay tribute to all those at the club, especially the players, all of whom have worked so hard for success, some for four years or more. Individuals will always come and go, but the legend that is Celtic continues.'

But his words meant little to the supporters. Furious fans had gathered at Celtic Park chanting for the heads of McCann and Brown and holding high banners calling for the two to go. The last time that was seen at Celtic Park was four years earlier – when McCann himself helped remove the old and despised board. McCann must have wondered what had all gone wrong to find himself the focus of so much hate. But, if he did, he didn't stop to worry too much about it. He had other things on his mind. The share price of Celtic had tumbled with the news of Jansen's departure and he didn't want it falling any further as he began putting into place the final pieces in his jigsaw which would see him sell out after only one more season.

He had to keep the share price high and the club's accounts looking healthy. Bidders were already on the horizon and, with this latest revolt by the fans, talk of takeovers before he was ready for them was not something McCann desired.

Brian Dempsey had already hit the headlines over suggestions that he was ready to move in. He denied this, saying he only wanted to ensure that McCann kept his promise not to sell out to any big outside investors but would offer his majority shareholding to the Celtic fans first.

Within two weeks news was out that Dempsey was having talks with Simple Minds pop star Jim Kerr – a lifelong Celtic fan. Kerr made no secret of the fact that he backed Dempsey and he also had the money to help out if it ever came to it. He said: 'I want to talk to some of the people who can help put the club back into Celtic hands. I'm here to encourage a movement that hopes to see the future of Celtic in the hands of the people it belongs to.' Kerr also spoke of his support for Willie Haughey.

The potential for a 'Green Dream Team' was there – and it was going to stay. And there was the odd addition, including Celtic and Scotland legend Kenny Dalglish who, even at this stage, had more than a keen eye on what was going on at Celtic.

But McCann had his own ideas. He had to acknowledge the media speculation but in doing so he used the opportunity to hammer home his own message. He said: 'I would not forgive myself if I said let's get out of here and do something easier and forget about all the aggravation. I think that would be a mistake. It would also be unfair. You have to have a proper plan and I think I would let the club down if I just walked away now.

But he kept his options open adding: 'If something better for the club came along I'd have to consider it and the board would decide. Should there be something better for Celtic Football Club, and it is good for all parties, it would be bad business not to look at it. But that has not happened.'

It was already happening but McCann was quite happy to wait – and hopefully watch the share price rise along with the multi-millions of pounds in profit that this would mean for him personally.

THE one thing the fans weren't happy to wait for was the appointment of a new manager to replace Wim Jansen. As the summer of '98 drew to a close there was still no one on the horizon although there had been plenty of speculation and promises from Jock Brown that a new manager would be in place before the season began.

A total of 25 names was debated in the media, among them many of the great players and managers of the decade. When the announcement came some weeks later there was laughter and mocking. Then there were tears and fears. The man McCann and Brown had searched long and hard for turned out to be a 62-year-old Slovakian coach who had previously been sacked by Aston Villa – Dr Jozef Venglos. He was immediately dubbed 'Dr Who?' but the fans had no choice but to place their faith in him as the season began for the champions.

First, though, there was the traditional raising of the league flag for the first home game of the season at Celtic Park. And that turned out to be an occasion even McCann hadn't banked on.

As the small, almost timid-looking figure of the managing director and chairman of this great club walked out into the cauldron of the massive new 55,000 seater stadium he had helped build, he was booed by the home supporters.

It was the ultimate embarrassment for McCann and one which left him looking stunned and almost speechless. But his arrogance this time helped him through when he went ahead with the unfurling, after making his point to the fans that this was a day to celebrate and be proud, so let him get on with the job in hand. The supporters did. They had made their point and made it forcibly in the way only they could. It was their stadium, not his. And a lot of their money had gone into the building of it despite many wishing instead it had been spent on players and greater success on the field.

If they thought that would change with the arrival of Venglos they were wrong and it was Venglos himself who dropped the clanger by saying it.

After only eight weeks in the job Dr Jo came out with the stunning news that he believed Celtic could retain the championship without having to spend more money on new players. Only two days after losing an early season midweek league match 1–0 to St Johnstone, Venglos told a pre-match press conference the news the fans didn't want to hear.

Venglos said: 'I am accepting that we are missing a player who has been scoring goals but we have players in the team who have been scoring goals in the past. I am still believing in the players who have shown before that they have the ability to score. I am patient. I am believing in them.' The fans weren't so believing, not while rivals Rangers continued to spend millions on new players, licking their wounds over having lost the championship and vowing to prise it back.

Celtic went on to drop a point at home to Hearts the next day in a 1–1 draw.

After just eight games played in the league, Celtic found themselves five points adrift of leaders Rangers.

Worse was to come as Celtic took an early exit from the Champions' League and then from the place they were later given in the UEFA Cup. Rumours familiar to Celtic fans from previous days started to be heard once more as reports appeared of clashes between Venglos and Brown.

The chants were again being made for the blood of McCann and Brown. This time something had to give. It was Brown.

During the September AGM McCann and Brown were booed and jeered but it was Brown who received the loudest abuse. The shareholders approved a move to increase the shares a hundredfold and move on to the official Stock Exchange, but they did not approve of Brown.

McCann said he was going on the end of the season to some applause but he added: 'Neither Mr Brown nor I intend to resign at this time.'

But Brown was living on borrowed time. After yet more reports of fall-outs – including one with Celtic star Paul Lambert – and just after that European exit, Brown was 'sacrificed' by McCann.

The axe fell in early November the day after Celtic had hammered Dundee 6–1. At the press conference called to announce the news McCann said: 'Unfortunately, in recent times, it became clear to the board that, despite Jock's best efforts, progress in some important matters and issues had been compromised. This may have had an adverse effect on the current football atmosphere and the backing of our supporters.

'I have discussed these matters with Jock and he accepts this. Consequently, he tendered his resignation. Jock appreciates that there is a feeling within the massive Celtic support that a significant change is desired. He acknowledges that, under the circumstances, he requires to be the major part of this change.

'We had a heart-to-heart talk and we realised this. We are not in a blame game here, but things had happened and Jock was at the centre of the football operations and so he was affected. It was an extremely difficult situation and he felt that resigning from his post was the best thing to do for everyone concerned.'

Brown still said he would walk out of Celtic Park for the last time 'with my head held high' and seemed not to accept all the blame being attached to him.

He said: 'I thought about everyone involved, including myself, and decided it was right for all parties that this happened. There has been a combination of circumstances at work here and all of them were taken into consideration when this decision was reached.

'There is no question that I made mistakes in some matters. I think my biggest error was in my judgement of how the press should be handled. However, there were other matters which I believe worked out for this club, but I don't intend to go into all of the details because that is not why we are here. I am not going about apportioning blame or looking for praise.'

The move did go some way to appeasing the fury of the fans but McCann knew that wouldn't last. Right now his main focus of attention was once more on the shares and keeping them high. Two things were helping him do that – a better performing team and increased speculation over who was lining up with the mega-bucks to bid for his shares.

TEN

Double Act

IT was just before Christmas that Kenny Dalglish and Jim Kerr decided to make Fergus McCann the offer of a nice Yuletide present.

What they had in mind was around £29 million in hard cash. That was treble the investment McCann had made in Celtic almost five years previously. But yet again McCann was definitely not in the Christmas spirit. He dismissed the offer out of hand as being far too low.

His valuation of Celtic, taking into account the share price, assets and all other ways of manipulating figures, was nearer to £120 million, which meant he could expect £60 million. The true value of the club – which fluctuated only by a small amount – was actually around the £80 million mark, which would still see McCann walk away with around £40 million.

The Dalglish and Kerr consortium now had the financial clout of leading international bank, Bankers Trust. They were represented by Kilmarnock-born financial wheeler-dealer Jim McAvoy who helped put the deal together. He did not dispute the true value of the club, which had grown into one of the biggest in the UK and certainly with the best stadium and club ground capacity about to hit 60,000. But his consortium believed £29 million for McCann's controlling interest was very fair and said they wanted to spend the balance of the money they were prepared to invest on new players and creating a soccer academy to rear more home-grown youngsters in a style which the modern game demanded. The fans loved the idea. McCann despised it. He wanted all that was coming to him and, in his eyes, that meant the £40 million he was already banking on.

The media reports over the interest pushed the share price higher. McCann was revelling in that while people like Brian Dempsey, who had already spoken with Kerr previously, was cringing. It was the reason he had urged Kerr to hold off with any bid.

Looking back Dempsey said: 'Jim is one of the finest guys you may meet, one of the plainest people I have had the pleasure of speaking with on many subjects. The problem with the plan he and Kenny had was that they were impatient, they wanted to get on and they thought I was too laid back but that wasn't the case and I tried to stress that to him.

'I was sitting back. I was waiting on the share price tumbling. I was waiting on that but they were becoming concerned and decided to move. I met the chap Jim McAvoy and I also told him my route was to wait – let things drift to see Fergus more and more backed against a wall and see what he was going to do.

'He told me that they couldn't do that, that they needed to get on. I said the offer at that time wasn't helpful because all it did was push up the share price to the advantage of Fergus, which would make him harder to deal with. Now who benefits from that? If Celtic Football Club did I'd be saluting it, but the club doesn't benefit. Individuals benefit and one individual in particular, whoever it might be. It is not against Fergus. It is not just because it is him.

'If he decides to sell his share to the fans it will make it much more expensive to buy and the club gains nothing. Fergus gains. For a man who, at the outset, said he was prepared to take £1million in profit after five years, he then looked to walk out with £30 or £40 million. It's obscene. The Celtic community in Scotland pitched in to make this club – it's absolutely wrong that any one individual should go out with that kind of profit.

'I'm not bitter in the slightest but I think it has been a strategic error on the part of Jim and Kenny, but Jim Kerr is a Celtic fan and his heart is in the right place.'

WITH the Kerr and Dalglish consortium returning to their London-based financial backers, McCann's attention now turned to another attack.

This time it was his long-running battle with the SFA and Jim Farry in particular over the botched-up registration of Celtic's Portuguese striker Jorge Cadete.

It may have dragged on for almost three years but McCann was determined to win this one and he was getting closer to his goal.

After threatening to take the matter to UEFA and then, possibly, to court if necessary, which could have brought sanctions on the club as it's against the sports rules to take your own football association to court, the SFA launched an internal inquiry. But that inquiry cleared Farry. McCann was furious and continued his campaign which then led to an independent inquiry into the handling of the player's registration, and cost him a place in the Scottish Cup semi-final against Rangers in April 1996 which Celtic went on to lose 2–1.

The inquiry would be held before arbitration expert John Murray QC, the former Lord Dervaird, at the end of February.

McCann was already on record earlier that month

speaking out against the SFA, yet again, despite that fact that the independent inquiry was about to start. He said 'The tail should not be the controlling force in Scottish football, but that is what we have got.

'Preservation of blazers, benefits, perks and being part of the club should not be the driving force. It should be what the customer is clamouring for and that is quality on the field.

'I think the SFA have a function but their biggest function should be the non-professional game and that should be supportive rather than controlling. Scotland versus Estonia is no longer the driving force on a Saturday afternoon here and 60,000 people will not go to see that game.

'What are the priorities of the SFA? Is it about preserving votes and having a national showpiece stadium which is used three or four times a year at huge cost to clubs, or is it about developing the grass roots of the game? Where are all these indoor centres that money could have bought?'

Strong words and demeaning to the SFA. Both sides then went into the Cadete inquiry with guns blazing and many people believing that McCann had bitten off more than he could chew in what was one of the longest and most bitter disputes involving a Scottish club and the overlords of Scottish football. But they were wrong.

In one of the most astonishing climbdowns in Scottish football history, the SFA conceded defeat before the inquiry was over and, even more remarkably, publicly blamed their chief executive Jim Farry for his 'failures' in the handling of the case.

The SFA also took the unprecedented step of issuing a letter of apology to Celtic over the matter and agreed to make an offer of compensation. The soccer chiefs then suspended their top official – the highest executive in Scottish football.

McCann then announced to the astonished media corps

which had gathered that he wasn't stopping there. He wanted Farry sacked.

The Celtic chief executive said: 'Mr Farry's failure on more than one occasion to properly register Cadete, and the serious implications for Celtic arising, leaves the club in no other position than to ask for the office bearers of the SFA to recognise that Mr Farry's position is untenable.

'I cannot see a rational explanation for his actions. I am not claiming there was any malice, but there was intent. In the overall interests of Scottish football, and to maintain its reputation for fairness and justice, this case demonstrates clearly that Mr Farry cannot be allowed to hold and exercise such powerful authority. I would deny that there is any vendetta on my part.

'For the sake of Scottish football, I would like to see this thing over now because it is taking too long. We have spent too much time to press an issue that should never have required so much of our time. It's not a matter of this being personal.

'After all the effort that has gone into this I would hope that all other clubs recognise that what we did was absolutely necessary. Frankly, I'm glad it's all over. I was just doing my job to make sure that Celtic were treated fairly. This is not a Celtic issue any more.'

Celtic were to receive substantial compensation, believed to be around £100,000, with as much again paid by the SFA for the club's legal and other expenses involved in the case.

Farry was shattered. He believed he had followed the rule book and the beleaguered SFA chief executive insisted that he was entitled to defend himself in a further inquiry promised by the association office-bearers which would consider his position.

But that next inquiry by the SFA executive committee turned out to be nothing more than a farce. They had already decided to sack Farry and they confirmed that after their meeting just over one week later.

The frightened-looking faces of the men now in control of the SFA lined up to announce their verdict. Leading the pack was former Celtic director Jack McGinn, who had been booted out when McCann took over the club five years earlier. Because McGinn was the President-elect of the SFA, McCann agreed to keep him on in a 'consultancy' role so that he could continue on the SFA executive committee. The fact that he was obliged to McCann and Celtic meant he hadn't taken part in the initial inquiry. But now he sat uncomfortably at the head of the table, having announced he had temporarily taken over Farry's position. His voice quivered and he stuttered as he tried to answer questions.

It was easier to read from a prepared statement which said: 'The Scottish Football Association advises that, following the suspension on full pay of its chief executive Mr James Farry, the decision has been taken to dismiss Mr Farry immediately for gross misconduct.'

The statement went on to detail aspects of the handling of the Cadete affair and outlined the reasons for Farry's dismissal as:

> His conduct during the period of investigation of the resignation by an SFA sub-committee.
> The preparation of the SFA's case for the arbitration.
> His testimony during the arbitration.
> The period since his suspension.

The SFA statement added: 'We do not intend to make further comment on the reasons for Mr Farry's dismissal, for reasons of confidentiality.' It concluded: 'It has been a very difficult period for the association and the recent events should not be allowed to cloud the work which Mr Farry has undertaken on behalf of the association and, indeed, Scottish football. There are many positive things which can be attributed to Mr Farry over these years which should not be forgotten.'

Farry announced he was considering legal action after his nine years at the SFA had come to such an ignominious end. He said: 'I do not accept I have done anything wrong and I intend to clear my name.' But the issue was to end there. A substantial pay-off would be made to Farry which would also buy his silence and that, in turn, of the SFA on the matter.

There were many Farry supporters but there were probably many more in Scottish football who had waited a long time to get rid of him. Even some of those on the SFA's committee structure had quietly been burrowing away over the years helping to push forward the knives which would eventually stab Farry in the back. But, while he was looking over his shoulder, McCann's knife had struck him in the chest.

THERE had been no love lost between Farry and McCann and, now that he had won his case, the Celtic chief executive skipped on home to play happy families.

Former lawyer, wife Elspeth was expecting the couple's third child. They already had daughters Ishbel (3), and one-year-old Juliet – who were yet to realise the significance of the media intrusion to their south-side mansion in Pollokshields.

The press was full of speculation about his marriage and there were frequent calls at their house asking questions. Elspeth would often appear in a white dressing-gown, telling reporters that she did not speak to the press.

Fergus asked for his home and family life to be respected as private and totally detached from Celtic Football Club.

He would then issue denials and appeals about his private life through Celtic Football Club's public relations mouthpiece, Peter McLean, denying the rumours and asking for his private life and that of his life at Celtic to be kept apart.

He turned to journalists he trusted – who were few and far between and were mainly based at the tabloid *Daily Record*'s news section who joined him at Sunday mass – and poured out his heart about his 'delightful' marriage.

The *Record* printed 'scoops' showing McCann and his children to the world, expounding what a great person he was. But, on the back pages, they lambasted the man.

In one of the news reports it referred to Fergus: 'When he closes the door of his massive villa, the turmoils and traumas of being the Parkhead boss are left behind.

'Inside, he steps into a world where he is barely heard above the din of his two doting little girls climbing all over him. This is the Fergus McCann the world never sees. And few who witness his waspish, hardball image would believe that the uncompromising chief executive could be so wrapped up in a world outside of football.'

The words were enough to make many Celtic supporters cry tears in their pub pints at teatime.

Yet McCann and his wife did hold their 'togetherness' together. They even spoke about it. Elspeth (36), and McCann (57), told how they had survived as a family 'despite the stresses of Fergus's job'.

Elsbeth said: 'The key is to keep family life and work life totally separate. When Fergus walks through the door he is our Fergus, our star man, irrespective of what is going on outside. Fergus is able to switch off when he comes home and I really admire him for that.'

Fergus said, to the same tabloid: 'If I have had a very aggravating day, I come home and my life is completely different. I talk to Elspeth and she gives me all the support I need. Having worked as a lawyer she knows what it is to have a high pressure job.

'I have to say it is not easy to switch off, but, to be honest, I don't know what I would do if I didn't have

Elspeth and the family. Having a family really gives you a completely different perspective on things. And it creates a huge, necessary balance in your life.'

About the boos at the unfurling of the League flag he said: 'It was disappointing for me and and for the other people who worked so hard at Celtic. What happened didn't diminish my pride and satisfaction at being there. I was very heartened and touched by the volume of calls I had from the people at the time. It's not all one way.'

Meanwhile, as McCann and his wife quietly celebrated his personal victory over Farry and the SFA, the bid for his controlling interest was resurfacing from the Dalglish and Kerr consortium.

It seemed the deal-seeking duo and their backers would not take no for an answer. Not that McCann ever expected them to. Neither did he want them to. They helped keep the share price healthy.

The media again was full of speculation and debate. And then enter the not-so-long-departed manager Tommy Burns – then boss at English strugglers Reading. He went on record backing his old buddy Dalglish in the new takeover bid. It was his view that Dalglish would 'be the man to carry the emotions into a new era at Celtic Park'.

Burns continued: 'I think it's always been in Kenny's mind that Celtic were a club that should be right up there in the top echelons of world football. Maybe Kenny wants to put it right after leaving Celtic as a player. They were at the top at one time but dropped dramatically because different people never re-invested in it. Kenny might see that as the challenge to go back in there and take Celtic to the top.

'People say he's a chequebook manager but that's only because people gave him money to spend. They wanted something improved quickly and that means better players.

'Kenny has made mistakes like everybody else. There's no guarantee in the transfer market, but he's certainly got an eye for players and he knows the type he would need to bring to a club like Celtic. I think he would go out and bring in the best quality players. He'd strive for that and he's got a worldwide pool of people he deals with to get that type of player.

'I think anything would be possible for Celtic with the following they have and the backing they've given the club. They've put fortunes into Celtic and anything should be possible.'

BBC Scotland then helped keep the Dalglish and Kerr consortium in the headlines with a television documentary on the great debate.

Dalglish, Kerr, McCann, Haughey, Billy McNeill and others with a few words to say all featured in the programme.

Dalglish said: 'When it became public knowledge that there was a consortium, myself, Jim and Bono along with Jim McAvoy were told by 93 per cent of fans in a poll that they'd like it to happen, mostly because they thought we would bring something to the club and build on what's already there.'

For financial backers Bankers Trust, the input to get Dalglish on their team was to promise £20 million for the playing side and nearly £8 million for his pet dream of a soccer academy. Dalglish said: 'It's something I believe in. It doesn't guarantee that you're going to get players though, but it gives you a better chance of succeeding. If you can provide good facilities and, most importantly, good coaching for the younger players, then you must have a chance.

'I think another important aspect is that the money is there and available to enhance and improve the squad at the discretion of the manager, whoever was going to be the manager at that particular time. If you're asking 60,000 supporters to put their hand in their pocket and come out and support then I think they deserve better than to be selling their best players. Unfortunately Celtic is seen as a money club which is disappointing when you think they've got the best average attendance in Britain.

'Out of courtesy when we were going to put the offer to Fergus's advisers, I phoned Fergus and told him that it was genuine and told him that I was part and parcel of it, it wasn't just something which anyone had written about in the press. I told him that we would at all times treat him with respect. I hoped that we'd get a little back from him but, at the end of the day, he never spoke to any one of us.'

But McCann was having none of it although he appeared rattled and at times arrogant as he stuttered: 'I don't see him as an investor frankly. I don't see any evidence of that in the proposal. We never got anything in great detail at the beginning that could be presented to the board. We eventually did and we informed the board and we dealt with it. I thought they'd got the message that it was up to them to make a coherent, specific bid which would be dealt with. In its present form there is no point in them doing so.

'We've got the right kind of people at Celtic now. We've got the right kind of board, we've got the right kind of set-up and we've got the right kind of backing. We've now got to get on to the next step. We're probably the only club in Scotland that makes a profit right now. That means we're able to invest money in the following year and I think that's important. We're not working for the bank like the club used to do. We'll be able to invest more and more in the playing side which is what the supporters are most interested in. We've got to build a major training centre, which the club intends to do. But we want to do it right. By maintaining its present momentum it's going to be able, I think, to get bigger on the field as it gets bigger off the field. And a lot of that, of course, is to do with good management.'

The fact that the club was in profit had a lot to do with the fact that McCann didn't authorise any great amounts of money to be spent on players – a bone of contention with Burns for a long time.

And being in profit looked good for the books and the financial state of the club as a company which, in turn, made it even more attractive in terms of business and share prices – and that was what mattered to McCann. The higher the share price the higher the millions he would eventually walk away with. In other words, even selling out his controlling stake to the fans would mean them funding his departure rather than funding the club as they did when the first shares came on the market.

Countering that claim, McCann said: 'But the fans are also being given the opportunity to look back on the fact that it was a good investment in the past. I think you find that people who tend to buy into winners when, at the time, buying into what was a potential loser, are again looking to buy into a winner. Anyway, I think they would obviously make a decision based on their own objectives and not so much mine.'

But the favoured option for McCann was still to offer the biggest part of his 51 per cent stake to the fans – and sell the rest to fellow director Dermot Desmond. It's believed he had already made a pact with Desmond before Dalglish and Kerr came forward.

But Desmond would not want any more than 25 per cent of the club. Much more than that and he would have to make a formal bid for all the club's shares which is something he would not want.

It would also allow him to have a major say in how the club shaped up to the future but without having to take a public profile. He is already one of the least known of the Celtic directors despite having invested more than £4 million in the club.

What little is known about Dubliner Desmond is his colourful and controversial past and he no longer talks to the media because of it.

His business interests have spread worldwide from intriguing deals in Afghanistan to a luxury hotel complex in Barbados, a stake in London City Airport and a computer software technology business and mobile phone network in Ireland.

He hit the headlines in 1993 after a government inquiry into a Dublin land deal involving the main Irish telephone company. Desmond was strongly criticised in the report, which concluded he had benefited from the deal after he'd sworn an affidavit that he hadn't. It was after that public humiliation that the flamboyant Desmond refused to talk to the media and he retreated into a very private life.

Although he is now considered to be the new Mr Celtic with McCann's departure, Desmond might never have got involved at all if it wasn't through a chance meeting on a golf course near Dublin with a Lanarkshire publican.

Charlie Woods from Airdrie was caddying for his brother-in-law, English-based professional Robert Lee in the Irish Open at the time when Desmond was splattered over the Irish newspapers.

Woods didn't know who he was at the time. He said: 'We were in the players-and-guests VIP area after a round and Desmond overheard me talking. He heard the Scottish accent and asked me if I was a Celtic fan. I said I was and always had been and we talked a bit about Celtic and Old Firm matches. He'd never been to a Celtic and Rangers game and said he would love to go over and watch Celtic play.

'I didn't really think too much about it all. It was the next day when I was in the clubhouse and came down the spiral staircase. A table at the bottom had the Sunday newspaper laid out and there, on the front pages, was Desmond. I couldn't believe it. I had been talking away to this guy just the other day. I knew he was pretty rich from meeting him but I'd no idea he was a multi-millionaire.

'It must have been over a year later when I was president

of Paul McStay's testimonial dinner, just before the shares' issue, that I thought about him again. I approached Dominic Keane and told him of my conversation and said he might want to talk to the guy with a view to him investing in Celtic as he'd appeared to be a great, and very rich, supporter.

'Dominic got in touch with Desmond's financial advisers and the rest is history. I wouldn't want to think I am the one responsible for Desmond being at Celtic but it's funny how chance meetings like that turn out.'

Funny indeed, but it soon became no laughing matter as Desmond's power and control at Celtic Park began to grow (and it still is).

Dermot Desmond was also one Celtic director who was watching and listening despite the claims by McCann that he had no interest in the Dalglish and Kerr consortium.

Both he, and Allan MacDonald, the new general manager at Celtic Park, and McCann's last appointment in March 1999, are known to admire Dalglish and neither would rule out any future involvement of the football legend at Celtic.

MacDonald is a former British Aerospace director and lifelong Celtic supporter. The Ayrshire man moved in quietly at Celtic Park but he knew his work would soon be cut out for him.

ELEVEN

Speaking Out

AS new boss Allan MacDonald moved in, McCann was quietly moving out of Celtic Park.

His last appearance at the stadium he helped create was on Saturday, 3 April 1999. He took his seat in the directors' box for the last time and received some small applause from a few hundred fans around him. That was the only acknowledgement he got as he prepared to leave the country in order to escape paying massive capital gains tax when he eventually sold out.

McCann watched Celtic demolish Dundee 5–0. But he got up and left a few minutes from the final whistle. Few saw him go.

Two days later he had packed his bags and flown out of Glasgow Airport with wife Elspeth, daughters Ishbel and Juliet and baby son Malcolm.

They looked like any normal family. McCann was now just a husband and dad, although a very rich one. His interest in Celtic was almost over. He would still be in contact with the club and new boss Allan MacDonald until he sold his shares later in the year, but, for now, family life beckoned.

McCann's views on that were already recorded. He said: 'My wife is an only child and as for me, my mother never thought I'd get married. When I look at my children it puts life firmly into perspective.

'I don't know what I'd do if I didn't have Elspeth and the children. Having a family creates a necessary balance in your life. We are blessed with three healthy children and all the things we have.'

Before they left on a flight to Brussels, Elspeth said: 'When I married Fergus I knew we would be leaving Scotland when his time was up at Celtic. I'm really looking forward to it.' The couple were planning to make their home in Bermuda.

ALTHOUGH McCann had little to say on his five years of stress, turmoil and achievements at Celtic, the men who knew him well – and some not so well – had plenty to say.

Old Firm rival boss David Murray had crossed swords with McCann on several occasions but he also respected what he had achieved.

Murray said: 'I don't think the way he went about things in a purely professional business sense was wrong, but it was on the public relations side where he fell.

'His handling of Jock Brown was an example where it was obvious Fergus had listened to his advisers. But McCann's views were too many times purely for Celtic business motives and his own and he failed to realise that sometimes things aren't just for the short term interest of your club.

'During one season Celtic's television revenue was higher. When it was reduced for the following season he wasn't happy. Half the time I do stupid things for football reasons. I tend to let my heart rule my head when it comes to football whereas Fergus did it 100 per cent for business reasons.

'Talk is cheap and he has delivered, purely in a business

sense. He had his way of dealing with things and we have our way. It's a fact of life.

'I do charity work everyday and so do our players. We don't look for the press to be there. Fergus wanted to get the Celtic charity image through the media. Everything with Fergus was to create image.

'Fergus has also upset a lot of club chairmen because of his off-the-cuff remarks. There must be a respect between us all and I don't think Fergus appreciated that. I think sometimes he just spoke for himself.

'His agenda was completely different. I would never be brave enought to say I'd spend money on players and not do it.

'And to stand on the park after winning the Championship and be booed like he was would have gutted me. I don't know if I could have ignored that. If I had got that sort of reception I would have thought "what the hell am I doing here?" I like to think I would have adapted, adjusted and gone to visit and talk to the various supporters' bodies. As I've said before, I think he misjudged what he got into.

'We are all guilty of that one way or another, but I think Fergus was more so. Fergus said he would be open but he wasn't.

'He made a strong financial contribution to the club but I felt the longer he was there the more distant he became. I suppose he knew he was going and therefore didn't bother about how he was regarded by others.

'It was interesting to see how his media improved a bit after Jock Brown. Maybe he should have been more forthcoming before that.

'It will be hard to judge his success through anything other than trophies. The ground and the club are stronger and he should, quite rightly, be given credit for that. But it's trophies the fans want and measure success by. I think Fergus was right to go when he did. It was probably the right time, having established the stadium.

'I am not doubting what he has done but maybe the way he has done it. Sometimes you wonder if he was a true Celtic supporter because some of the decisions he made were purely financial and for him – not for the football club and its supporters. Only time will tell when they look back on his tenure at Celtic.'

FORMER director Willie Haughey popped up on radio praising his former boss. But he also expressed some criticism. Looking back over his term at Celtic and his clashes with McCann, Haughey said: 'Once all the major issues were out the way and things settled down we only had issues about the playing side, the football side, and one of my biggest bones of contention was my project to set up a soccer academy for the youth.

'It's something which we fell out over because nothing moved. I think it's been borne out because there's still not a spade in the ground and, basically, I was wasting my time. For five years there has been total lip-service to a Celtic Academy. We had drawings and planning but I just felt as though my time had been wasted.

'I don't know if Fergus ever had any notion, any real intention of going ahead with that. I don't think it was a priority and obviously that's been proved right as he's come and gone and nothing was done in relation to those facilities.

'I'll never take away from what Fergus has done and I appreciate that totally, and I think he is due every penny that he got, but I do believe that if you want to be a successful football club in the real sense then you don't have money in the bank as Celtic did while he was there.

'If you can tell me a football club that has won the European Cup and has money in the bank I would accept it but you can't. I don't think there is one. Real Madrid won the European Cup a couple of years ago and they have a £60 million overdraft. Even Manchester United, who may be an exception, are spending most of their profits on the stadium and new players, but that's football.

'Basically, Fergus was never really football-orientated as such. I always think he wanted the team to win but he always had to cut the cloth accordingly.

'There were occasions when I wanted to go the extra mile over his spending. I used to think there was a lack of common sense in not giving Cadete and Van Hooijdonk a little bit more, then you have to go and bring in somebody else who wasn't in the same class and have to pay them double.

'I just got the impression that most of my confrontations with Fergus would have been on small issues. On the bigger scale, on the football side, maybe we had different ideas.

'A lot of the time we were just paying pure lip-service and for a while I just accepted it, like over the possibility of joining the English Premiership.

'It would certainly have put Celtic in a league of their own in terms of Scottish football – wouldn't it? That's something which Fergus would've been remembered for if he'd gone with it.'

DOMINIC Keane was probably closer to McCann after the takeover than anyone else on the Celtic front. He was there from the first day after the rebels won until he walked out over the Haughey affair three years later.

He recalled: 'After me and Willie left I don't think anybody who had an alternative view was listened to at the club. I have got to say that in the last 18 months the atmosphere changed quite significantly within the club and that's not because Haughey and I left – it's because you need people within the club who have different points of view and are prepared to express those points of view.

'I honestly believe that if Fergus had operated a one-man show from day one without us he would not have lasted 12 months. And that is not to say that he was not a catalyst in many of the things – I'm not in any way trying to take away from what Fergus has achieved because there were a lot of positives as well – but he couldn't have come from Canada back to Scotland and operated on his own without a good team beside him, a team that also understood how the Celtic supporters' minds worked.

'It's always important to discuss and talk things through and get other opinions and I believe that there aren't enough people who are in there now who are prepared to sit down and discuss rationally without any other agendas what is the right way forward.

'I think that's one of the reasons that he was booed when we achieved the League Championship. It was a tragedy, an unbelievable situation and I think that the people around him didn't know or understand this whole Celtic ethos, that yes, you've got to have the business side, but you've also got to be seen in the public eye as being user-friendly too. I don't think that came through.

'And I think, therefore, that the removal of Jock Brown was inevitable. I don't think that there was any question or doubt that he was the wrong appointment – people said he was the wrong appointment from the beginning and he had to endure a year when relationships between its supporters and the club dropped to an all time low.

'Despite that I believe that if the board understood what the feelings of the supporters were then that would never have happened and I think it was just another indication that there was nobody in any way trying to control some of the things Fergus was doing. I think he was also trying to rush through a lot of things in his last year and that didn't help matters. He had his moments but I think things can only improve again now he's gone.'

ONE man who was glad to see the back of McCann was the same man who was instrumental in him coming over in the first place.

But Brian Dempsey believes the McCann he had first met was not the same man he later came to know and fall out with.

Looking back over the years Dempsey – who many believe is needed in some official capacity at the club – said: 'Things turned sour between us early on. We had some meetings and I was not happy. I recognised the kind of individual he was. I decided in my heart I wanted nothing to do with him. I knew he was there to exploit as much as he could the Celtic fans and take as much out of this as he could get. I knew from the things he told me and what others had told me that he would be totally ruthless with anyone and everyone. And the casualty list would be high. An American who must remain anonymous told me there would be bodies everywhere and of course the casualty rate a month before the changeover was phenomenal. People were destroyed in his path because he has no feelings for anyone other than the dollar, the almighty dollar.

'I found him obnoxious, insulting to people around him and disrespectful of other human beings. I can accept a lot of things but I cannot accept being nasty to ordinary people. Obnoxious to the extent he spoke to other people as if they were waiters, barmen, taxi drivers, I couldn't handle that, it really disturbed me. He is a man of no social grace, no personality and not many manners.

'He was incredible and said the most terrible things. He shocked me totally when he demanded a press conference which I advised him against. It was the September weekend at the time when he was harangued about having this press conference on the day of the Old Firm.

'It was the semi-final of the then Skol Cup – September '93 – and he said he didn't know the game was on. He continually handled everything like that badly. Everything had to be written out by his PR people, Barkers – he handed me something he wanted me to read out but I didn't and spoke my mind. After that Barkers always said to me – 'oh yes, Mr Dempsey, you go unscripted.' Everything had to be read from prepared notes by Fergus and he was caught out with loads of questions. When he said he didn't know that Celtic had an Old Firm game on the press hounded him for that. He was always given to saying things like that because, I believe, he doesn't care about what he says or the way people react to it.

'I think my biggest regret was believing in him and then finding out the truth. He was there more for himself than for Celtic. I didn't know that at the time. He said publicly he was only looking for a 10 per cent profit over five years and that made some of the press cuttings and I admired that.

'He said he wanted to see Celtic to go from strength to strength and he has tried many things over the past five years but it was all a mask. I also regret the way Celtic has become a stockmarket commodity. I speak to a few people and all they tell me is the price of their shares now. That's dangerous. But this will all go full circle and Celtic will need to become a footballing institution again and it's at that time people will see the dangers and folly of stockmarket manipulation and all the things we condemned the Kellys and Whites for in trying to take money out of the club and making profit out of Celtic. Fergus has succeeded in making many people fall for the same crime.

'Despite what some people think, I have no axe to grind. He offered me a directorship and I declined it. If I was prepared to be as mealy-mouthed as other directors he had I could have sat there all that time and worn the blazer and got the free trips but I turned that down because I didn't believe in it.

'I would love to say Fergus had done the most fantastic thing for Celtic, and he has done some good things and they will all be well recounted. But the fact remains that it's a stockmarket commodity with a whole host of problems. Many casualties on the way, human beings discarded for whatever reason, for whatever purpose, anything that you have to do to obtain your end, cannot be good.

'If I had put my money in with him it would be worth five times more today although I would be guilty of hypocrisy.

'My former business partner John Keane was taken in by him. John promised that he wouldn't invest. We both agreed that we wouldn't invest and then he went behind my back. He allowed it to be said that I didn't have the money to invest and yet he had to come to me to take the £1 million for his investment out of the joint company account which had £8 million in it at the time. I had helped make John Keane millions of pounds.

'He is the biggest disappointment to me – a much bigger disappointment than Fergus McCann. I knew Fergus McCann. I thought I knew John Keane. Now he sits with the green blazer on and watches the games.

'This club is in a more perilous position now than it was in 1994 because it will be leaderless – whatever kind of leader Fergus was he was a leader. It will be run by faceless men whose motives for Celtic are not Celtic motives, they are more likely to be personal, and whose purpose is to push up the share price and push up their own profitability. Meanwhile the people of the West of Scotland and the Celtic community there and beyond will continue to have to purchase season tickets, pay money and do other things to see Celtic attempt to become a football club again. It's much more perilous now than it was then because there are so many people involved and affected by the illness of greed.

'Fergus McCann was beneficial in some respects for Celtic Football Club, disastrous in others. The reputation of the club has suffered at home and abroad. The method and type of leadership was entirely unsatisfactory. The Celtic community strove to achieve great things with Celtic to bring a dignity to their own individuality which was reflected in Celtic Football Club – that dignity has been lost.

'In my eyes, and I think in the eyes of a great many people, Fergus will be remembered for walking out with millions of pounds in profit. Once the dust settles and it sinks into people what really has happened, that's how he'll be remembered.'

THERE was someone else whom many believed was a front-runner as sworn enemy of Fergus McCann. Jim Farry – the former SFA boss who was toppled from power at the so-called House on the Hill by the Celtic supremo.

Farry had said nothing since his departure due mainly to a confidentiality clause written into his £250,000 'golden handshake' contract with his former employers but, after pulling the strings at the SFA and the Scottish League for more than two decades, Farry was then digging the garden and decorating the house because he'd fallen foul of McCann and Celtic. Nevertheless, he did reveal his sadness over the loss of his job; he denied he had been made a scapegoat, and shared his hopes for the game.

In the Farry-speak he was often criticised for, he said: 'I suppose it's better from both the employer's point of view and the ex-employee's point of view that matters have been resolved amicably. It would be inaccurate to try to singularise 27 years in football administration.

'As far as being described as a scapegoat, that's for others to determine – but I didn't leave under a cloud. I wouldn't describe myself as bitter. My employers decided that my employment had to be terminated. I've no regrets. I worked with a good team at the Association and the League and I was proud to have been part of the developments which have come about and I'm supportive of those now in charge.

'I miss the involvement with my colleagues. But as for the pressures, stresses and strains – no, I don't miss that.'

Nor did he miss McCann. But, surprisingly, he didn't hate him either. In fact, he actually had admiration for the aggressive little Scots–Canadian millionaire.

In a refreshingly honest assessment, Farry said: 'I never held any personal bitterness towards Fergus McCann. How could I? I didn't know him personally. It's not as if we socialised and I really got to know him. I only knew him as the person who dealt with the Association regarding club matters for Celtic.

'I found him very focused, very singular and very driven. Football embraces so many different types of people with so many different personal interests and with an idiosyncratic view of life. It's a melting pot of emotions – an alchemist's dream, in my opinion. I found it difficult to familiarise with anyone in the game because I only had fleeting contact with them but I think the commitments McCann made to the club business structure were honoured in full and the programme he set out was achieved. Celtic, it would appear, required some form of leadership and there is no denying they got that through Fergus McCann. You can't fault anyone who sets targets and achieves them. He did well.'

TWELVE

So Long

BLOOD, sweat and tears were words used often to describe events surrounding Celtic during the stormy McCann years at the club. But none more so than the day which was to become one of shame at Celtic Park, a game which left McCann a furious fan abroad, although he was probably happier to be there.

Sunday, 2 May 1999, was the day when Rangers travelled to the ground of their oldest rivals looking for victory to secure the Championship flag. It was a day every Celtic fan relished. They believed the Bhoys – who had thrashed Rangers 5–1 earlier in the season – were more than capable of ruining the party for the Ibrox outfit.

But it was not to be. Rangers won 3–0 amid scenes of chaos and violence both on and off the field.

Rangers secured the league title on the ground of their most bitter rivals for the first time in more than a hundred years of their football feud and the night was scarred not only by defeat, not only by Rangers' title win, but also by the shame of both players and fans.

Stephan Mahe and Vidar Riseth were both sent off along with Rangers' Rod Wallace; Frenchman Mahe's response to the decision by referee Hugh Dallas, however, was to refuse to leave before finally being convinced and walking off in tears; on three separate occasions Celtic fans ran on to the field before being stopped by stewards; Dallas was hit by a missile and suffered a bloody head wound which required attention before he could continue.

Rangers were not entirely blameless: when the game ended, the Ibrox players went over to their celebrating group of fans and foolishly went into a mock huddle.

The season – McCann's last as owner of the club – had ended in shame and defeat. There was defeat again later that month when Rangers beat Celtic 1–0 in the Scottish Cup final at Hampden but at least there were was no repeat of the scenes at Celtic Park. Celtic were later fined £45,000 by the SPL for what became known as 'the shame game'.

AROUND the same time Celtic's shares were starting to drop and that was something which concerned McCann even more. Shares in football clubs do tend to flutter depending on results but, in this case, the drop over a relatively short period was high so McCann decided it was time for a boardroom comeback. He was, after all, still in charge even if he was now a tax exile. One way around the strict tax rules governing entry into the country during the first year was to hold a board meeting outside of the UK. And that is what he did. McCann summoned the Celtic directors to a crisis board meeting in Dublin. He stood to lose around £5million as the club's share price plummeted by more than 10 per cent.

It was the first time in Celtic's history that a board meeting was held outside of Scotland. The dramatic move came after Celtic's share price tumbled from a high of around 340p to just 305p amid rumours of boardroom rifts and the loss of the league title. McCann had expected to walk away with around £40 million when he sold up but the price tumble was wiping millions from his personal fortune.

Although he based himself in the south of France for tax reasons, McCann was technically still the chief executive, with Allan MacDonald not officially due to takeover until 1 July. And McCann proved he still cracked the whip over those he had left behind: he was reported to be furious at the way MacDonald, the man he appointed to replace him, has handled certain affairs, like splashing out to keep top striker Henrik Larsson, and settling differences with Mark Viduka. MacDonald was also keen to see Kenny Dalglish back – despite McCann snubbing the former Celts hero only months before.

Celtic plc directors Brian Quinn, Sir Patrick Sheehy, Kevin Sweeney and Eric Riley were still McCann's men but MacDonald had the powerful backing of Dermot Desmond, the Dublin-based millionaire likely to as the club's main shareholder.

Points were made but so too was peace, and the share price stabilised. There was, however, one point on which McCann *did* lose. Kenny Dalglish – although, in fact, the following month McCann was reported to be 'chuckling', some £375,000 richer with the arrival of Kenny Dalglish at Parkhead. That was the increase in his shareholding when the news of Dalglish's appointment as technical director was confirmed.

Allan MacDonald had risked his all on King Kenny. MacDonald was a close friend of Kenny's (golfing buddies) and had pushed his case, in which he was supported by Dermot Desmond. Fergus was reported to have given in to MacDonald, with the warning that if it all went wrong the responsibility would be his – a clear implication that his head would roll in the event of failure.

Even at the last moment the deal was in the balance because the Celtic board were furious over a leak to a tabloid that Dalglish's former Liverpool colleague John Barnes would come with the package as team coach – despite his having no coaching experience. According to the club's plc vice-chairman Brian Quinn, McCann ruled himself out of the voting that brought Dalglish back to Parkhead.

Quinn said: 'Fergus felt it right that he should not take part in these decisions as we were the people charged with the job of taking the club forward. He did have his views, as you would expect of Fergus, but after he expressed them, he left the decision to us. In my opinion he behaved punctiliously. We began by engaging a head-hunting firm to produce candidates, and they came up with about thirty names.

'We then worked hard to reduce that and eventually we were left with four. Every one of them was interviewed by us, and that included non-executive directors as well. In the end our decision was unanimous. Talk of a faction against Dalglish was just not true. Sir Patrick Sheehy and I were supposed to be part of that faction. I just cannot say with any more emphasis that this was not the case.

'Kenny has an enormous reputation, but among all the other things about him is his attention to the development of young players. I know a lot of football people down south and they all say the same thing about him.

'If you remember what happened when he went to Newcastle United, you can see his way of thinking. Kevin Keegan scrapped the reserve team at St James's Park, but the first thing Kenny did when he got there was reinstate it. He is convinced that the development of youth is a vital part of the progress in any club.'

FOR Fergus McCann the idea of youth emerging from a football academy at the club was not new. He had allowed former director Willie Haughey to work away on the dream for a considerable time but McCann appeared to have no real intention then of forking out the cash for it. Now that he was selling up, the idea was back. But it was back on his terms.

The grey September clouds hung over Parkhead as McCann jetted into Glasgow for the announcement of the sale of his shares. The media had been summoned to report at Celtic Park for an 11a.m. press conference. But, once again, confusion reigned. The teams of sports, news and business journalists who descended on the stadium were turned away and told to come back at 1.30p.m. – McCann's plane was late.

It was to be McCann's final appearance as the first, and possibly the last, person to hold a controlling interest in one of Britain's biggest and oldest football club's. The man with the bunnet who shuffled into Celtic Park with a frown five years before now waltzed into the boardroom with a suntan and a smile. And he had every reason to be chuckling. Around £40 million worth of reasons to be exact. He was now putting his 50.3 per cent controlling stake up for grabs and the £40 million was what he expected to walk away with after investing £9 million when he took over.

Not a bad return. Some thought it 'obscene', particularly as none of that profit would go back to the club. It was all heading for McCann's pockets, but he didn't care what people thought. He told the packed media gathering: 'I feel quite good about the situation. More than that, everybody else has done better than Fergus McCann.'

His explanation for that comment came from the fact that fans who bought shares when he first floated the club stood to make the same percentage profit but without having had to have worked for five years at the club.

Flanked by Allan MacDonald and a rotating replica of the European Cup – a reminder of former glories – he was relaxed about the massive return on his investment.

He added: 'Everyone who bought shares now sees them worth a lot more than they paid for them. They did not pay out the same sort of money as I did – and they did not work for five years on a fairly modest salary as I did. And I have not taken any dividends.'

An indication of his intention to mix it a bit and to enjoy, for once, a news conference, came at MacDonald's expense. McCann turned to his replacement at the club and said: 'I didn't have the £200,000 a year salary which Mr MacDonald has.'

At that point, MacDonald's face turned a shade of red and he forced a smile on to his lips. Staring at the table, he no doubt cursed under his breath.

McCann didn't stop there. He indulged in some more controversy by making a stinging attack on the new Hampden, his pet hate, and took a veiled sideswipe at Rangers – another pet hate. After 'five years which nearly blew my brains out', McCann said he thought Hampden was not just a great folly, but a great scandal. 'It has cost clubs like Celtic and many others very heavily, besides, of course, the taxpayer.'

He believed the needs of a national stadium could have been met by the existing stadiums at Parkhead and Ibrox, at which point he could not resist a financial aside on the Old Firm rival.

'I think I leave this club in a sound financial situation. The club has no debts, is beholden to nobody and is primed to move ahead. Unlike other clubs who have a win-at-all-costs policy, we have based ours on financial stability.'

He kept to his commitment of offering supporters the opportunity to buy shares. Under the offer of sale, priority would be given to existing shareholders and then to season-book holders resident in the UK and the Irish Republic. He estimated that the sale of his stake would leave 40 to 45 per cent of Celtic's shares in the hands of fans and other small-scale private investors. City institutions would control just over 22 per cent. He was offering them at £2.80 a share, a discount on the quoted price of £3.15.

McCann said: 'I have been approached by several parties interested in acquiring my entire shareholding, but I have declined to enter into discussions. Any such sale would probably not have incurred the costs of this exercise and, in my opinion, may have yielded a higher sale price than I will receive as a result of offering my shares for sale in this way.'

Up to 58,000 shareholders and season-ticket holders were offered by McCann a credit of £1400, interest free, to help pay for 500 shares each over one year. It also opened the door to major shareholders like director Dermot Desmond, who was the second biggest shareholder after McCann. Desmond and two other major shareholders – club director John Keane, and the Trainer family who had recently sold out their lucrative advertising business – had already taken almost 3 million of the 14.4 million of McCann's ordinary shares which were up for grabs. Along with 10 institutions, they had also underwritten the remaining shares if the fans couldn't afford to buy them, but that could have led to any great volume remaining being taken by companies – and McCann didn't want that. So to encourage the supporters to snap them up, McCann came out with the 'carrot' – the soccer academy.

That old chestnut was back and, under McCann's terms, it could become a reality. But only if the fans bought his shares.

He pledged to donate £1.5 million to Celtic to create the academy, cash which would be handed over by McCann in three installments, depending on the level of take-up of his offer. It was a move typical of the shrewd McCann but one which also opened him to accusations of 'greed' and 'exploitation'. Most sections of the media slammed him over the proposal and suggested the money should have been offered without the conditions attached. But it was like water off a duck's back. McCann was dictating the play right to the end and he didn't care what the others thought.

'I am happy I made the decision to come here and I feel better for it. The fact that I was able to make an impact in returning Celtic's standing in the eyes of the supporters is the key issue.

'Eventually you have to get a thick skin and realise that doing what is necessary is not always the popular thing. It's like a shirt against a suit, the shirt will always win and the shirt is the side taken by the media. You have to accept that and do what you think is correct; you have to have a very strong focus and not be diverted from that otherwise you'll be cut to pieces.

'I did what I could. I'd like to have seen Celtic further ahead, but looking back they probably achieved the progress we set out to make. I don't have a lot of hair now but I didn't to start with. Five years is plenty.'

Five years was indeed plenty. Plenty for McCann and plenty for many who had to deal with him. But, as Fergus John McCann quite literally headed off into the sun which was setting in the west behind Bermuda and Canada, the legacy of his five years was about to unfold. And the faithful left behind were once more holding their breath.